# JOY AT WORK WORK AT JOY

## Living and Working Mindfully Every Day

JOAN MARQUES, Ed.D.

BOOKS FOR ALL THAT YOU ARE

**PERSONHOOD PRESS**

Joy at Work, Work at Joy
Copyright © 2010 by Joan Marques

For permission or book ordering information contact the publisher:

Personhood Press
PO Box 370
Fawnskin, CA 92333
(800) 429-1192
Fax: (909) 866-2961
*www.personhoodpress.com*
*info@personhoodpress.com*

Library of Congress Control Number:  2009938262

ISBN: 9781932181531

Printed in China

Book and Cover design by: 1106 Design

# Foreword by Marshall Goldsmith

## Joy at Work, Work at Joy: Living and Working Mindfully Everyday
### By Joan Marques, Ed.D.

I often use Buddha's teaching in my work. For example, Buddha suggested that his followers only do what he taught if it worked in the context of what was happening in their own lives. He encouraged people to try out what made sense, do what worked for them, and "let go of the rest." Similarly, I teach my clients to ask their stakeholders for suggestions, listen to these ideas, contemplate what's been offered, try out what makes sense, do what works, and let go of what doesn't.

In her motivating and encouraging book, *Joy at Work, Work at Joy*, Joan Marques offers suggestions in the form of inspiring quotes from some of the greatest minds that ever lived. Each of these pearls of wisdom is offered in order that one might live and work mindfully every day. Supporting each quote is an accompanying action item and a story or point to ponder relative to the quote. You may choose to ponder every point and try every action offered, or you may not. Either way, these suggestions can be looked at as gifts. If you can use the gift, use it. If the gift doesn't strike a chord for you or if it doesn't feel relevant for your life right now, put it someplace safe and "let it go."

Thank you, Joan, for this great gift of daily guidance!

~ Marshall Goldsmith—million-selling author of *What Got You Here Won't Get You There, Succession: Are You Ready?* and the upcoming *MOJO*.

# From the Author

Gautama Siddharta, better known as the Buddha, once said, *"We are shaped by our thoughts; we become what we think. When the mind is pure, joy follows like a shadow that never leaves."* There is a lot of truth in these words, and you don't have to adhere to any specific religion, ideology, culture or generation to understand it.

This is a book of positive thoughts, carefully written over the course of three years, and especially focused on working people. We all work in different environments: some of us travel a lot, others work in the same office or factory for decades; yet others work from home, telecommute, or shift jobs regularly. Regardless of who and where you are at this moment, you will find yourself in this book. It is written for people who want to take more ownership of their lives—people who realize that positive thoughts lead to higher awareness, which leads to constructive actions, followed by improved circumstances, a better living and working environment, and, ultimately, a better world. Every great movement has started with one good intention from one wakeful person. *You* could be that person, and this book could steer you in the right direction.

*Joy at Work, Work at Joy* is not a book that you read from cover to cover in a day or a week. It should be read in small sections daily, because it entails a quote, an action plan, and a point to ponder for each day of the year. Some of the action plans are specific, and others are deliberately kept general to leave room for your own interpretation, according to what is going on in your life at the time. The points to ponder are either presented as elaborative thoughts on the quote, or age-old stories from all over the world.

This is a timeless book that transcends boundaries. People from all beliefs, cultures, mind-sets, preferences, ethnicities, or other classifications will relate to it well. It is a great gift to others, but even more to yourself, and can be used at various stages in your life, even after you have retired. Changing your world and your circumstances starts with changing yourself for the better. You just took the first step. Cheers!

— *Dr. Joan Marques*

January

# January 1

**GUIDING QUOTE:**
*Life is a promise; fulfill it.*
~ MOTHER TERESA

**ACTION:**

I am fulfilling my life's promise by lending a smile to all those who may have a hard time finding one of their own. I radiate my good intentions, show that I care. This way, I enrich my own spirit and those I encounter.

**POINT TO PONDER:**

The promise of life can only be fulfilled through our own actions. That is the power we have. If we decide to give in to misery, mean-spiritedness, or tedium, we will dread our circumstances, and the fulfillment of life's promise will be bleak. If we decide to be courageous, loving, and mindful, we will enjoy every step of the journey, and the fulfillment of life's promise will be grand! We are the sculptors of our life, and we can create either a beautiful sculpture of togetherness by showing that we care, or a desolate monument filled with egotistical "I"-ness. We make the promise; we fulfill it.

# January 2

**GUIDING QUOTE:**
*Make the best use of what is in your power,
and take the rest as it happens.*
~ EPICTETUS

**ACTION:**

I use my power by offering my assistance where it is not expected—helping out a colleague, assisting a stranger, taking my loved ones out to dinner tonight. By making their day, I am making mine as well.

**POINT TO PONDER:**

An old couple got curious when they saw a young man dressed in working clothes passing by their cottage every day with a spade and a briefcase. After two weeks of watching, they decided to take a stroll before the young man arrived to see what he was doing. They came upon a rocky area and saw that he had been digging a trench. When he arrived, the old lady asked what he was doing and what he had in the briefcase. The young man explained, "I'm learning how to dig a good trench because the job I'm being interviewed for later today says that experience is essential, so I'm getting the experience. And the briefcase…it's got my lunch in it." He got the job.

# January 3

### GUIDING QUOTE:

*One must not attempt to justify [aspirations and judgments],*
*but rather to sense their nature simply and clearly.*

~ ALBERT EINSTEIN

### ACTION:

Instead of justifying others as if they are part of a different world, I try to see the mirror of myself that is everyone around me. I seek to understand before wanting to be understood. I keep in mind that each of us has our own reality, and that such is what makes the world a beautiful place.

### POINT TO PONDER:

Two monks were washing their bowls in the river when they noticed a scorpion that was drowning. One monk immediately scooped it up and set it upon the bank. In the process he was stung. He went back to washing his bowl and again the scorpion fell in. The monk saved the scorpion and was again stung. The other monk asked him, "Friend, why do you continue to save the scorpion when you know its nature is to sting?" "Because," the monk replied, "to save it is my nature."

*(Adopted from John Suler, "Zen Stories to Tell Your Neighbors")*

We should remain true to our nature and respect that of others.

# January 4

GUIDING QUOTE:

*It is the greatest mistake to think that man is always one and the same. A man is never the same for long. He is continually changing. He seldom remains the same even for half an hour.*
~ GEORGE IVANOVITCH GURDJIEFF

## ACTION:

I cherish the thought of continuous change. I am subject to change on a constant basis, and so are others. It would be shortsighted of me to think that anything or anyone is the same as last week or even yesterday. I embrace change, because it is part of living.

## POINT TO PONDER:

Oftentimes, we do not realize that we're constantly changing, because we are part of ourselves all the time! But we erroneously expect others to remain the same, and get disappointed when we find out the opposite. It is important to be aware that we change through all the influences we encounter—books we read, people we meet, circumstances we face, impressions from every place—our minds develop as a result of these encounters.

# January 5

**GUIDING QUOTE:**

*An ant on the move does more than a dozing ox.*

~ LAO TZU

**ACTION:**

My actions speak louder than my words. I perform to the best of my abilities and do not get distracted by others who do not practice what they preach. I set a good example because I know it is for the betterment of everybody, as well as for my inner gratification.

**POINT TO PONDER:**

A Chinese teacher used to labor with his pupils even at the age of eighty, trimming the gardens, cleaning the grounds, and pruning the trees. The pupils felt sorry to see the old teacher working so hard, but they knew he would not listen to their advice to stop, so they hid away his tools. That day the master did not eat. The next day he did not eat, nor the next. "He may be angry because we have hidden his tools," the pupils surmised. "We had better put them back." The day they did, the teacher worked and ate the same as before. In the evening he instructed them, "No work, no food."

# January 6

*A friend is one before whom I may think aloud.*

~ RALPH WALDO EMERSON

## ACTION:

I am a friend to those around me without expecting anything in return. I do not abuse information that is shared with me in trust. Even if not confidentially shared, I do not use information from others for my own gratification or to deliberately hurt them. I realize that I can only find real friends when I am one.

## POINT TO PONDER:

How many of us are afraid to speak our mind anymore because someone may use our own words against us? How often have we heard of or experienced cases where individuals distorted others' statements with mean-spirited intentions? Finding someone with whom we do not have to be on guard is a virtue. Being the one with whom others do not have to guard their words is nobility.

# January 7

**GUIDING QUOTE:**

*You think you lost your horse? Who knows, he may bring a whole herd back to you someday.*

~ CHINESE PROVERB

**ACTION:**

I do not allow material loss to daunt me. If I lose any property, I consider it to be for a good reason. If I miss an opportunity, a better one will emerge.

**POINT TO PONDER:**

One day, the stallion of an old farmer broke its fence and ran away. The neighbors said, "That's so bad!" The old farmer just said, "Maybe." The next day, the stallion returned with three wild fillies. The neighbors said, "That's great luck!" The old farmer said, "Maybe." The farmer's teenage son went out to break one of the new horses. It bucked him, and he broke his leg. His neighbors said, "How unfortunate!" The old farmer said, "Maybe." The army then came around, conscripting young men to fight in a war. Because of the broken leg, they didn't take the farmer's teenage son. The neighbors said, "How fortunate!" The old farmer said, "Maybe."

# January 8

## GUIDING QUOTE:
*I had no shoes and complained, until I met a man who had no feet.*
~ INDIAN PROVERB

## ACTION:
I am grateful today. Grateful for all that I am. Grateful for all that I have. And grateful for all that I can be for others. I am fortunate to be here—to be able to read this, or hear it being read to me. I am fortunate for being part of the world—a miracle of its own. There are many who have less than I have. I try to find ways to help them and rejoice for the opportunity.

## POINT TO PONDER:
We take too many things for granted and sometimes complain about little things that do not work out as we thought they would. Complaining is one of the easiest things to do. There is so much to complain about. But there is also so much to be thankful for. Unfortunately, many of us prefer to focus on our mishaps and take our blessings for granted. This might be a good moment to consider changing our attitude in that regard.

# January 9

## GUIDING QUOTE:

*It is better to have less thunder in the mouth and more lightning in the hand.*

~ APACHE PROVERB

## ACTION:

Instead of talking all the time and not doing much, I show the world who I am! I lead by example, even if I am not an official leader of anyone else but myself. I do the things that I have postponed for a while, and get organized where I was not. I work systematically until the day is over, and then I retreat with a sense of accomplishment.

## POINT TO PONDER:

It seems that many places encourage thunder in the mouth. Assertive people often steal the show. However, the greatest talkers are oftentimes the weakest doers. It might be wise to observe people for a while before drawing a conclusion on their actual qualities. Those with thunder in the mouth usually have little lightning in the hand, and those with lightning in the hand often have little thunder in the mouth.

# January 10

## GUIDING QUOTE:
*The moon moves slowly, but it crosses the town.*

~ AFRICAN PROVERB

## ACTION:

I do not allow myself to panic when things do not happen as rapidly as I want them to. I do my very best to accomplish whatever I can, but I also practice patience where it is needed. I keep in mind that some things require more time than initially anticipated. I do not let that discourage me.

## POINT TO PONDER:

Haste is everywhere around us. But haste doesn't always invite good outcomes. While we may not slack unnecessarily, we should always consider the fact that there may be unforeseen hurdles that might delay our plans. However, as long as there is progress, there is hope. Sometimes we appreciate the outcome of an effort better if there were setbacks on the way to achieving it. It is hardship on our way to paradise that helps us value the destination even more.

# January 11

## GUIDING QUOTE:

*In the end, we will remember not the words of our enemies, but the silence of our friends.*

~ MARTIN LUTHER KING, JR.

## ACTION:

I am not upset by comments of those who dislike me. I am not disturbed by lack of support from my friends in times of need. I accept them as they are, because they are connected to me.

## POINT TO PONDER:

There is an old Sufi story of two friends who traveled together. One night they came across a town with prostitutes. One friend wanted to indulge in physical pleasures, while the other tried to change his mind. Both wanted their way, so one went with a prostitute, while the other went to church. Meanwhile, the friend with the prostitute became regretful of his foolishness. The friend in church kept thinking how lowly his friend was. Then an earthquake demanded both their lives. In heaven, the remorseful fool was awarded over the one who thought his friend to be lowly. Thinking ourselves superior to others is the gateway to hell.

# January 12

**GUIDING QUOTE:**

*Work relieves us from three great evils: boredom, vice, and want.*

~ FRENCH PROVERB

**ACTION:**

I am grateful to work. I am the driver behind my actions, my co-workers are my family at work, our customers are the purpose we perform, and the universe makes this possible. My work has meaning.

**POINT TO PONDER:**

A large corporation hired a team of cannibals to reorganize the workplace under one condition: no eating of employees. A few weeks later the HR manager called a meeting with the cannibals: "I am satisfied with your work so far, but one of the secretaries is missing. Anyone know anything?" All cannibals shook their heads. After the boss left, the cannibal leader said to the others angrily, "OK, which one of you ate the secretary?" One hand hesitantly rose in admission. "You fool," said the leader. "For weeks we've been eating managers and no one noticed anything, but you had to go and eat someone important!"

# January 13

## GUIDING QUOTE:
*The mind is everything. What you think, you become.*
~ BUDDHA

## ACTION:
I remain calm and quiet, even when challenged. Positive or negative thinking are both choices. I choose positive.

## POINT TO PONDER:
A farmer needed to work his field, but his plough was broken. He decided to ask his neighbor, Murphy, who lived four fields away, knowing that Murphy finished his work early on. The farmer started to walk to his neighbor. After the first field he thought, "I hope Murphy has finished his work, otherwise he can't help me out." As his concern grew, the farmer thought, "Perhaps Murphy's plough is old and almost broken. Then he will not loan it to me." After another field, "Murphy has always been a hard one. He might just not want to help me out." Upon arriving at Murphy's farm, the farmer's mind was so clouded that he thought, "That Murphy was always a mean one. He won't help me just out of spite." He knocked on Murphy's door and yelled angrily, "Murphy, just keep your stupid plough!"

# January 14

GUIDING QUOTE:
*The only true wisdom is in knowing you know nothing.*
~ SOCRATES

## ACTION:

Because I know nothing, I realize that I have no reason whatsoever to be arrogant. There is so much I do not know, and whatever I think I know became obsolete the moment after I learned about it. I open myself to learning, and I keep in mind that teachers come in various shapes and sorts, human and nonhuman.

## POINT TO PONDER:

Humility is not as easy to practice anymore these days, because our society encourages us to swank about our skills and capacities. The loudest mouths seem to get all the glory, and that sends a message of discouragement to all who believe in humility. However, it is also important to know that there is a long-term outcome to everything. Superciliousness is a hard act to maintain, and ultimately crumbles. Humility remains intact and opens the way to continuous learning.

# *January 15*

*Happiness is when what you think,*
*what you say, and what you do are in harmony.*

~ MAHATMA GANDHI

## ACTION:

I decide to be happy. I refrain from lying, cheating, or deliberately hurting others. I consider my words carefully, but I remain honest. Responsible truthfulness is possible. I do not partake in gossip, even if it doesn't hurt anyone else directly, because it stains my spirit.

## POINT TO PONDER:

There is freedom in being truthful. This sense of freedom starts within and radiates to others. Authentic behavior is simple behavior. It detangles us from the web of hypocrisy that social behavior sometimes demands. It prevents us from having to remember too many behavioral patterns applied to too many environments and individuals. Most importantly, it enables a well-earned and peaceful night's sleep.

# January 16

### GUIDING QUOTE:

*The greatest gift you can give another is the purity of your attention.*

~ RICHARD MOSS

## ACTION:

I give the greatest gift by listening. I listen to my family and make sure that I am not caught in too many distracting activities. I listen to my colleagues and do not get carried away by my ambition. I listen to my pet and do not ignore this true friend of mine. I listen to those around me, because they are precious.

## POINT TO PONDER:

If we think of the most common sentence we speak everyday when we encounter others, "How are you?" and we expect no more than "Fine, and you?" our intention is often not to hear more than that. We cannot even start imagining that someone would want to really tell us how they are. Why not change that? Why not show that we really care? Our body language can add meaning to our most common question. We can give more attention. It will enrich those around us, ourselves, and our connection.

# *January 17*

GUIDING QUOTE:

*[A]s we let our own light shine, we unconsciously
give other people permission to do the same.*

~ NELSON MANDELA

ACTION:

I set an example and exude a pleasant mood and an active attitude today. I work hard and practice kindness. I demonstrate my good intentions by offering my help where it is not expected.

POINT TO PONDER:

Once there were two true friends, Ndemi and Jinjo. Ndemi was rich, and Jinjo poor. Yet, they looked very much alike and did everything as if they were brothers. They traveled together, and one day, when Ndemi was in dire need, Jinjo came to his rescue, helping him to escape death and find his life's happiness. The friends soon separated, but their mutual lights kept shining for one another. Some time later, Jinjo got in trouble, and was facing an almost sure death. Ndemi sensed his friend's trouble, and traveled to Jinjo's village. He rescued his friend, and they were reunited.

# January 18

### GUIDING QUOTE:
*He that can have patience can have what he will.*
~ BENJAMIN FRANKLIN

## ACTION:
I realize that patience is almost outdated in today's hurried society, but that it provides me with an advantage if I practice it when and where no one else does.

## POINT TO PONDER:
A martial arts student went to his teacher and said earnestly, "I am devoted to studying your martial system. How long will it take me to master it?" The teacher's reply was casual: "Ten years." Impatiently, the student answered, "But I want to master it faster than that. I will work very hard. I will practice everyday, ten or more hours a day if I have to. How long will it take then?" The teacher thought for a moment. "Twenty years."

*(Adopted from John Suler, "Zen Stories to Tell Your Neighbors")*

Patience is a virtue that can only be taught through time.

# January 19

## GUIDING QUOTE:
*We are all in the gutter, but some of us are looking at the stars.*
~ OSCAR WILDE

## ACTION:
I focus on the positive. I am a stargazer. How beautiful is the sky! I imagine myself high up there. How great to be able to dream! How wonderful to have thoughts! I like dreaming. My mind is mine, and the freedom of my thoughts is the thing no one can take from me. I look at the stars and determine my path to them. My life is a promise.

## POINT TO PONDER:
It is all in our hands to get depressed or feel uplifted. While we cannot prevent ourselves from being less positive on some days, we can still choose to remain mostly joyful. The greatest predicaments are conquered by a sense of purpose. Unfortunately, many people fail to define their purpose and find their goal. Do not be one of them. Finding your purpose is a matter of turning inward and examining your interests. What excites you? Where is your star?

# January 20

**GUIDING QUOTE:**

*Optimism is the faith that leads to achievement.*
*Nothing can be done without hope or confidence.*

~ HELEN KELLER

**ACTION:**

I am an achiever, so I release the hopeless feelings that troubled me before. I accept the gift of each new day with the gladness and confidence of a child, and take it as it comes. If I encounter a windfall, I am grateful. If I encounter disappointment or challenge, I understand that it is up to me how I deal with it. I remain hopeful as long as I live.

**POINT TO PONDER:**

Hope and confidence are topics that have been lauded and condemned equally. However, what is life without a positive personal perspective? How do we dare anything if we do not hope for a good outcome? How can we face even the slightest challenge without some confidence? The great ones we now revere would not have become what they are without hopes. Nobel prize winners, inventors, great minds, artists, builders, and teachers: they all succeeded thanks to their hope and confidence.

# January 21

## GUIDING QUOTE:

*The pessimist sees difficulty in every opportunity.*
*The optimist sees the opportunity in every difficulty.*

~ SIR WINSTON CHURCHILL

## ACTION:

As I make the most of my life, my optimism is tuned on high. While I am not reckless, I mindfully accept what the day offers, and perceive it in the right light. I do not take setbacks personally, but see them as means to make me stronger and more determined on my way to achieving my goals.

## POINT TO PONDER:

Even if we are optimistic by nature, there is always a chance for partners, friends, or colleagues to drag us down with their gloomy perspectives. We should not get upset at them for being weak sometimes. Everyone has highs and lows, and that is OK. Instead of becoming upset with others, we could analyze the options and decide for ourselves that we will choose the opportunity viewpoint. This is how excellence is born.

# January 22

## GUIDING QUOTE:

*If your desires be endless, your cares and fears will be so too.*

~ THOMAS FULLER

## ACTION:

The things I really need are few, and most of the things I want are only infused in me by external influences or my own greed. Therefore, I carefully examine my motives. I do not want to be driven by cares and fears.

## POINT TO PONDER:

There is an African tale about the spider, Anansi, Firefly, and Tiger. Anansi, always trying to outsmart everyone, was invited by Firefly to go egg hunting. Firefly led the way, and they soon arrived in the egg field. Firefly opened his wings to shed light, but each time Anansi grabbed the eggs, stating, "This one's mine. I saw it first!" Finally, Anansi's bag was full, and Firefly flew off without one egg. Trying to find his way back in the dark, Anansi stumbled upon a house that turned out to be Tiger's dwelling. Tiger let him in, boiled the eggs, and ate all with his family. Anansi did not dare to complain, and quietly sneaked out in the early morning. His endless greed brought him endless fear.

# January 23

## GUIDING QUOTE:

*The difference between perseverance and obstinacy is that one comes from a strong will, and the other from a strong won't.*

~ HENRY WARD BEECHER

## ACTION:

I keep myself strongly aware of the difference between perseverance and obstinacy. Why be obstinate and make my surroundings and myself unhappy? I have a choice, and my choice is to exude perseverance to all who are close to me.

## POINT TO PONDER:

Perseverance moves ahead, while obstinacy remains stationary. Perseverance is future-oriented, while obstinacy stares at the past. Perseverance elicits willpower, strength, optimism, and drive, while obstinacy elicits anger, frustration, gloom, and depression. Perseverance motivates others, while obstinacy turns others away. Where do you stand?

# January 24

## GUIDING QUOTE:

*How inexpressible is the meanness of being a hypocrite!*
*How horrible is it to be a mischievous and malignant hypocrite.*

~ VOLTAIRE

## ACTION:

I am not a hypocrite. I review my behavior and apply honesty and fairness toward those who surround me. I realize that some people are habitual hypocrites and engage in crass politics to get ahead. I do not try to change them, and I am kind to them anyway. Even if their hypocrisy hurts me, I maintain my correctness, because my nights are undoubtedly calmer than theirs.

## POINT TO PONDER:

Hypocrisy is one of the many behaviors that have been encouraged by our society of class, hierarchy, and influence. Those who want to get ahead at any rate will engage in hurtful practices toward others. However, they also pay the price sooner or later when their conscience starts speaking up.

# January 25

**ACTION:**

I maintain my trust in the world and see my friends, colleagues, and family members as the honorable, wonderful individuals they are. I forgive those who engage in hateful practices toward me. I realize that their behaviors do not characterize the entire group.

**POINT TO PONDER:**

The few drops of the ocean that are dirty can become cleansed if the major share of the ocean is clean. If, in any environment, the majority of people are empathetic and embracing, there is a great chance that those with the malignant mentality will convert or exit. Yet, the opposite is just as true: if, in any environment, the majority of people are mean-spirited and rejecting, there is a great chance that those with a good mentality will either convert or exit.

# January 26

**GUIDING QUOTE:**

*No people is fully civilized where a distinction is drawn
between stealing an office and stealing a purse.*

~ THEODORE ROOSEVELT

**ACTION:**

Inadmissible taking is stealing in any case. I do not steal. I am alert of my attitude toward taking anything that is not mine.

**POINT TO PONDER:**

Stealing is a dangerous act. If we feel undaunted when taking a small office item with us, we will gradually feel undaunted in taking larger items. It has become so easy—almost acceptable—to take small things: a pen, some paperclips, or a notebook. But taking the company's stamps is equally unethical to taking the company truck. The often-used silencer, "Everybody does it," is no justification for anything that is fundamentally wrong. If we strive toward a sense of equality for human beings regardless of their rank, we should also understand the sense of equality in stealing something small versus something big: the character deficiency remains the same.

# January 27

## GUIDING QUOTE:

*To spare oneself from grief at all cost can be achieved only at the price of total detachment, which excludes the ability to experience happiness.*

~ ERICH FROMM

## ACTION:

I open up myself for love. I give my care and concern to those around me, and welcome the warmth they have for me in return. I realize that loving can cause grief. But love is worth risking that pain. I am human, and therefore I give and receive affection.

## POINT TO PONDER:

Detachment should be applied only to a healthy degree. Human beings are not islands. They co-exist with others. They are interconnected. Interconnectedness brings about vulnerability. We get used to loved ones, and grieve when they leave. Yet, we should be able to move on, for we are connected, but still uniquely ourselves. Our happiness can be disturbed, but it will be restored again, for life is an ongoing chain of growing, which involves hurting and healing.

# January 28

## GUIDING QUOTE:

*Silence is the true friend that never betrays.*

~ CONFUCIUS

## ACTION:

I partake in the interactions with my surroundings, but refrain from speaking for the sake of speaking. I honor silence, and embrace it as a second nature. I learn most from listening, whether it is to others or to the silence around me. In silence, I think and focus better on my purpose in life. I face myself and accept who I am without fear. Silence is my friend.

## POINT TO PONDER:

Silence has many faces. It can be comfortable or loaded. But it is up to us to be at peace with it. Some people have grown accustomed to constant noise. They fear the quiet, because they fear their thoughts. Rather than face themselves, they are constantly on the run from themselves. When you make a friend of silence, you start appreciating the wealth inside yourself, for silence draws that out.

# January 29

## GUIDING QUOTE:

*You must not fear death, my lads; defy him, and you drive him into the enemy's ranks.*

~ NAPOLEON BONAPARTE

## ACTION:

I stand tall in the adventure of life. I am my own personal champion. I know my qualities and value my being. I do not fear failure. I do not fear any kind of defeat, because defeat is an opinion that I do not share. I am brave and stand tall, for myself and those who rely on me.

## POINT TO PONDER:

Death is not necessarily a literal interpretation; it can represent failure of any kind. Conquering fear may be one of the hardest things to do, especially when we are traumatized by a previous occurrence. Yet, the sense of victory can only be achieved if we dare to face our fears and laugh at them. The key is to recognize our fear and find its roots. That is how we can address the problem. There is nothing wrong with laughing at our fears and ourselves, as long as we grow responsibly.

# January 30

*It is not easy to find happiness in ourselves,
and it is not possible to find it elsewhere.*

~ AGNES REPPLIER

## ACTION:

I turn inward and savor my source of happiness. I know that this inner source is not always easy to find, especially on days when things are not well with or around me. Yet, I have the ability to find happiness within.

## POINT TO PONDER:

In old China there was a water bearer who toiled everyday uphill with two pots hanging from a stick laid across his shoulders. One pot was perfect and always delivered the full amount, but the other pot was cracked and only delivered half the amount of water. The cracked pot was unhappy with himself. He told the water bearer that he felt inferior and embarrassed about his flaw. The bearer said to the pot, "Did you notice that there are only flowers on your side of the path, but not on the other pot's side? That's because you water them as we walk by. Thanks to you, I can pick these beautiful flowers and decorate my table. Without you there would not be this beauty to grace the house."

# January 31

## GUIDING QUOTE:

*What is uttered from the heart alone, will win the hearts of others to your own.*
~ JOHANN WOLFGANG VON GOETHE

## ACTION:

I do not speak hurtful things, but look for ways to be honest in as gentle a manner as possible. I am aware that openness and authenticity are appreciated by all, if not immediately then surely in the long run.

## POINT TO PONDER:

Arrogance is one of the major hurdles in speaking honestly. Many parents or supervisors think that their children or subordinates do not have the right to all information. But people have emotional intelligence. They can sense when you withhold information from them, and they do not appreciate it. Communication is a powerful tool, and it can overcome the most complicated problems when aptly used. Honesty is scarce, but we can end that scarcity.

February

# February 1

### GUIDING QUOTE:

*A man cannot be comfortable without his own approval.*

~ MARK TWAIN

## ACTION:

I look at my current circumstances and consider my living conditions, my job, and the social groups I am part of. If I approve of my circumstances, I improve them. If I do not approve of my circumstances, I work on a change. Today.

## POINT TO PONDER:

A wealthy father took his son on a trip to the country to teach him appreciation for their affluence. They stayed two days in the home of a humble farming family. On the way back, the father asked his son, "What did you think of the trip?" The son replied, "Very nice, Dad." The father asked, "What did you learn?" The son responded, "I learned that we have one dog in our house; they have four. We have a fountain in our garden; they have a stream with no end. We have lamps in our garden; they have the stars! Our garden goes to the edge of our property; they have the entire horizon as their backyard! Thank you, Dad, for showing me how poor we really are."

# February 2

*He who has injured thee was either stronger or weaker than thee.*
*If weaker, spare him; if stronger, spare thyself.*

~ WILLIAM SHAKESPEARE

**ACTION:**

I do not keep grudges. I eliminate senses of disappointment, anger, or fear toward those who have done me wrong. They, too, were my teachers.

**POINT TO PONDER:**

Many of us are consumed by feelings of anger toward parents, supervisors, or friends because of the way they treat us. Sometimes these others are aware of our feelings, but oftentimes they are not. When they are unaware of our feelings, we are the only ones suffering from our negative sentiments. Maintaining vengeful thoughts will cause us psychosomatic symptoms. Why allow that? It is better to consider the lessons learned and cherish them as opportunities for growth during the rest of our lives.

# February 3

## GUIDING QUOTE:

*Talking much about oneself can also be a means to conceal oneself.*
~ FRIEDRICH NIETZSCHE

## ACTION:

I refrain from talking about myself unless absolutely necessary. I realize that talking about myself does not necessarily mean telling the truth about myself.

## POINT TO PONDER:

Those who talk about themselves often do themselves grave injustice: they prevent themselves from learning from others. Self-ingratiation is rarely a beneficial act. It takes up the space of useful interaction, and it arouses a sense of repulsion in those who listen, regardless of their polite smiles. While some Western societies seem to encourage assertiveness, there is still a valuable distinction between aimless boasting and truthful sharing. Good listeners and wise people can detect this distinction immediately.

# February 4

### GUIDING QUOTE:
*If one advances confidently in the direction of his dreams,*
*and endeavors to live the life which he has imagined, he will*
*meet with a success unexpected in common hours.*
~ HENRY DAVID THOREAU

### ACTION:
I focus on the purpose of my life, so I use confidence, dreams, living, and success as my guides. I determine what success is to me, and live up to it.

### POINT TO PONDER:
To laugh often and much,
to win the respect of intelligent people
and affection of children,
to earn the appreciation of honest critics
and endure the betrayal of false friends,
to appreciate beauty, to find the best in others,
to leave the world a bit better,
whether by a healthy child, a garden patch;
to know even one life has breather easier
because you have lived.
This is to have succeeded.

*(Ralph Waldo Emerson)*

# February 5

## GUIDING QUOTE:

*So long as a person is capable of self-renewal they are a living being.*
~ HENRI FREDERIC AMIEL

## ACTION:

I engage in self-renewal because it is important on my way to higher awareness. I do this with increasing devotion. Old, downgrading thoughts need to go. I make the experience that is life more gratifying for all those I can reach: my family, friends, colleagues, and others in the wider circle of my existence. My renewal spawns a renewal in others.

## POINT TO PONDER:

Self-renewal does not have to be a complicated process. It can be done in many simple ways, depending on what you consider important: praying, keeping a journal, talking to different people, reading insightful literature, visiting spiritually illuminating places, allowing yourself some quiet time for reflection, practicing yoga or another rejuvenating exercise; the options are numerous. Self-renewal is invaluable if you want to mature without regrets.

# February 6

*I have learnt silence from the talkative, toleration from the intolerant, and kindness from the unkind; yet strange, I am ungrateful to these teachers.*
~ KAHLIL GIBRAN

## ACTION:

I am grateful for all lessons learned, so I change my aggravation toward those who have taught me wise behavior through their foolishness. Today, I honor them for who they are—my teachers.

## POINT TO PONDER:

Our real greatness lies in learning and, at the same time, forgiving those who taught us painful lessons. Gratitude is not always an easy emotion to generate, because the devastation that some people have brought about in our lives can be tremendous, and working up gratitude for devastation requires tremendous self-transcendence. Yet, until we forgive and start appreciating those hard teachers for their lessons, we will not have fully mastered those lessons.

# February 7

## GUIDING QUOTE:

*You already possess everything necessary to become great.*

~ CROW PROVERB

## ACTION:

Greatness looks different to everyone. Knowing that, I move toward the greatness I want to achieve by serving as much as I can. Wherever I can, I lend a hand. However I can, I make things happen. Whatever I can, I do to brighten the lives of those around me. I am content when I know they are. I am satisfied when I know I have given my all in whatever it is I consider my calling.

## POINT TO PONDER:

Education, mentorship, reading, traveling—all these activities can only contribute to greatness if we let them. It takes our own genius to apply our experiences in a way that distinguishes us from others who do not. Many people have had all the opportunities in the world, yet failed to answer the call of human greatness. Human greatness lies not in being world-famous, but in positively contributing to the quality of life of even one other living creature.

# February 8

## Guiding Quote:

*For the friendship of two, the patience of one is required.*

~ Indian Proverb

## Action:

I choose to live in harmony, so I will release any grudge I hold toward others. Why strain my soul? Why not positively surprise them, now that they least expect it? Today, I give them a token of my understanding, forgiveness, and friendship.

## Point to Ponder:

Long ago, in China, there were two friends, one who played the harp skillfully and one who listened skillfully. When the one played or sang about a mountain, the other would say: "I can see the mountain before us." When the one played about water, the listener would exclaim, "Here is the running stream!" One day, the listener fell sick and died. The first friend cut the strings of his harp and never played again. He had lost his most appreciative audience.

# February 9

**GUIDING QUOTE:**

*A short saying oft contains much wisdom.*

~ SOPHOCLES

## ACTION:

I keep my statements short and sweet, so that they are readily understood and convince my audience of the value I attribute to them. By being brief, I demonstrate that I took the time to think on what I wanted to say and how I wanted to say it. This is the greatest honor I can give.

## POINT TO PONDER:

Being brief requires much more preparation than going on at length, but it makes an infinitely deeper impression. So many of us recall meetings we attended where someone talked at great length without really coming to the point and without considering the whereabouts of his audience. Such individuals are rude and disrespectful. While they may not even realize it as such, they do not consider others important enough to take the time and phrase their statements concisely. What these individuals should realize is that they harm their own image by speaking aimlessly, for others will avoid them when and where possible.

# February 10

## GUIDING QUOTE:

*In critical moments even the very powerful have need of the weakest.*

~ AESOP

## ACTION:

I consider the reality of interdependence. I know I need others if I hope to perform better and learn more. I learn from everyone.

## POINT TO PONDER:

The powerful have a tendency to only use the weak in critical moments, and then forget the support they received as soon as they are where they wanted to be. Rich and powerful individuals, companies, and countries often use weaker ones for their own advancement and then forget to share the rewards fairly. Hate and war will persist in the world along with this short-sighted ignorance of empathy. Changing this condition is in the hands of each and every one of us. It is important to know that companies, countries, and continents are increasingly becoming interrelated. The reliance of all parties on one another becomes more obvious every day. This can be a beautiful reality, when abuse and neglect are consigned to the history books!

# February 11

### GUIDING QUOTE:

*There are four ways, and only four ways, in which we have contact with the world. We are evaluated and classified by these four contacts: what we do, how we look, what we say, and how we say it.*

~ DALE CARNEGIE

**ACTION:**

I pay attention to all four contacts listed above, and specifically focus on the following three today: what I do, what I say, and how I say it.

**POINT TO PONDER:**

The four contacts, what we do, how we look, what we say, and how we say it, are foundations upon which we are measured by our societies. Unfortunately, many societies lay too much emphasis on the appearance factor, and too little on the other aspects. While concern about how we look is indeed an important one, it is also the source of much pain and suffering in the world. People discriminate on basis of looks, especially considering the fact that we only have limited influence on that factor. We cannot change our race or gender, so how we look is a given to a large extent. We should think on that.

# February 12

*If all fools could fly, the sun would be eclipsed forever.*

~ DUTCH PROVERB

## ACTION:

I forgive myself for any foolish behavior I may have engaged in. While I realize that this does not mean that I will never again be foolish, today I refrain from foolish behavior.

## POINT TO PONDER:

We have to consider that even the most prominent among us have their own foolish behaviors that they are not too proud of, and their own dark corners that they would not like to display. The best we can do when we have done something we regret is to reflect on it, learn from it, and move forth. Dwelling on a sense of embarrassment will only rob us from our natural confidence and make us fearful of undertaking any new initiatives in the future. Making mistakes is a part of growing. Everybody is a fool sometimes.

# February 13

## GUIDING QUOTE:

*Freedom and love go together. Love is not a reaction. If I love you because you love me, that is mere trade, a thing to be bought in the market; it is not love. To love is not to ask anything in return, not even to feel that you are giving something—and it is only such love that can know freedom.*

~ JIDDU KRISHNAMURTI

## ACTION:

I present my attention, affection, and concern without expecting anything in return. My feelings of care and concern are genuine. My love is for free, and it sets me free.

## POINT TO PONDER:

How great it is to love without even knowing that we give it, simply because it is our nature. Freedom in love—how beautiful the thought! How important, also, to examine our motives when doing something for others. Are we genuine? Are we really not expecting any favors in return? Is it not enough to feel the fulfillment that giving brings without eroding it with expectations?

# February 14

**GUIDING QUOTE:**

*I've missed more than 9,000 shots in my career. I've lost almost 300 games. Twenty-six times, I've been trusted to take the game winning shot and missed. I've failed over and over and over again in my life. And that is why I succeed.*

~ MICHAEL JORDAN

**ACTION:**

I accept my failures as gateways to my successes. I am grateful for my failures because they cure me of arrogance and of taking my blessings for granted.

**POINT TO PONDER:**

Success lies in our belief about ourselves. Individuals and companies are increasingly celebrating their failures. At Intuit, a business and financial management solutions provider, employees even earn awards for excellent failures. This encourages them to examine how they can progress from the point of failure. They hold "postmortems" in which they analyze lessons learned, and keep track of new, more successful applications of projects that had initially failed. They believe that the only real failure is the one you fail to learn from.

# February 15

*Sometimes you must be cruel to be kind.*

~ English proverb

**Action:**

I am firm to myself and to those I love, because I want the best for us. I withhold what is negative to our well-being.

**Point to Ponder:**

Sometimes one has to deny others something they desire to make them better. If our child, spouse, friend, or colleague asks us a favor, we have to review whether this is to his or her advantage. It may initially seem like a contradiction or an act of control, but it makes a lot of sense! If a drug addict asks us for money to purchase drugs, we may be considered cruel to withhold it, but we are actually being merciful, because we want to help this person gain control over his or her addiction. If our child asks permission for a sleep over with friends who are irresponsible, we are being kind to refuse, even though we may be seen as cruel at that moment. Communication is important. Explain, and it might be understood.

# February 16

## GUIDING QUOTE:

*You cannot be lonely if you like the person you're alone with.*

~ WAYNE DYER

## ACTION:

When I am alone I am not lonely, because I appreciate my own company. There is a world of wealth in me to explore. There are so many thoughts to be thought, reflections to be reflected upon, and songs to be sung within me. I can only love others if I love myself.

## POINT TO PONDER:

There is a crucial difference between being lonely and being alone. Many people are surrounded by crowds and still feel lonely, while others are alone yet do not feel lonely. On our way to maturity, we go through many stages in which our self-perception can be damaged. We start disliking ourselves due to perceived failures, lost loves, missed opportunities, or poor looks. It may help to realize that all of us could find numerous reasons to dislike or like ourselves. Why focus on the bad? Loving yourself is not the same as self-ingratiation; it helps you accept yourself, which makes it easier for others to accept you.

# February 17

## GUIDING QUOTE:

*The mountains, rivers, earth, grasses, trees, and forests are always emanating a subtle, precious light, day and night, always emanating a subtle, precious sound, demonstrating and expounding to all people the unsurpassed ultimate truth.*

~ YUAN-SOU

## ACTION:

Ultimate truth lies in authenticity—being who I am, regardless of where I am. I do not wear different personality hats at different times, because I think that is hypocritical, even though society seems to demand it. People quickly distinguish genuine from phony.

## POINT TO PONDER:

As human beings we are connected to nature. However, we are also distinctive because of our ability to act in different ways under different circumstances. Is this an advantage? Not when it involves false profiling. That is deception, and it dims the natural light we could share with the mountains, rivers, earth, grasses, trees, and forests.

# February 18

## GUIDING QUOTE:

*Man...is a tame or civilized animal; nevertheless, he requires proper instruction and a fortunate nature, and then of all animals he becomes the most divine and most civilized; but if he be insufficiently or ill-educated he is the most savage of earthly creatures.*

~ PLATO

## ACTION:

I refrain from engaging in malice in any way. I educate myself in compassion and respect for all the living.

## POINT TO PONDER:

The greatest cruelties known so far on earth have been brought about by human beings, educated and ill-educated. Even highly educated human beings can be savages. The wars between nations may serve as an example. There is nothing divine in war, nor in any of its related actions. This may encourage us to contemplate on our civilization and some of the driving values we adhere to. How divine is any form of violence? We should make sure to refrain from becoming engaged in any industry or action related to violence.

# February 19

## GUIDING QUOTE:

*Most folks are about as happy as they make up their minds to be.*

~ ABRAHAM LINCOLN

## ACTION:

I am happy because I am content. I work at my goals, yet enjoy this beautiful life. Life is a gift that I cherish with those around me. Together we enjoy each other's light.

## POINT TO PONDER:

A man complained to his master, "I need help or I'll go crazy. We're living in a single room, my wife, my children, and my in-laws. The room is a hell." "Do you promise to do what I tell you?" asked the master. "I shall do anything." "How many animals do you have?" "A cow, a goat, and six chickens." "Take them all into the room with you, and come back after a week." A week later the man came back, moaning, "I'm a nervous wreck. The dirt! The stench! The noise! We're all going mad!" "Now, put the animals out," said the master. The man returned joyfully the next day. "How sweet life is! The animals are out. The home is a paradise, so quiet and clean and roomy!"

*(Adopted from Anthony de Mello, "One Minute Wisdom")*

# February 20

**GUIDING QUOTE:**
*Short is the joy that guilty pleasure brings.*
~ EURIPIDES

**ACTION:**

I examine the sources of my joy. I consider who is affected by my pleasures. If my pleasures are the guilty kind, I change them. I want to be proud of myself and my actions—even my pleasures.

**POINT TO PONDER:**

Guilty pleasures are numerous; an extra-marital affair, drug abuse, hunting without a need for food, laughing at others who are in less-fortunate positions, and cheating the boss out of his time, are just a few. The dubious value of these guilty pleasures is not only manifested in possibly getting caught, but even more in dealing with a troubled mind and a guilty conscience later on. When our conscience starts acting up, the pain subordinates any other penalty imposed. Facing the judge inside is harder than anything else. We should think on that before we engage in guilty pleasures.

# February 21

## GUIDING QUOTE:

*Happiness grows from the inside out.*

~ THICH NHAT HANH

## ACTION:

I look for the source inside, where my inner happiness resides. It is my own will and responsibility to be happy. By turning inward, I learn to find my path toward inner-happiness, and with that, the contentment to go through life with a healthy sense of detachment from everything that could discourage me.

## POINT TO PONDER:

A monk visited a master in his monastery. The master asked, "What do you seek?" "Enlightenment," replied the monk. "You have your own treasure house. Why do you search outside?" the master asked. The monk inquired, "Where is my treasure house?" The master answered, "What you are asking is your treasure house." The monk was delighted! Ever after he urged his friends, "Open your own treasure house and use those treasures."

*(Adopted from "101 Zen Stories")*

# February 22

## GUIDING QUOTE:

*Advice is like snow; the softer it falls, the longer it dwells upon, and the deeper it sinks into the mind.*

~ SAMUEL TAYLOR COLERIDGE

## ACTION:

My advice to others is soft and gentle. I do not know much, if anything at all. Therefore, I make kind suggestions when requested, rather than force my opinions and insights onto anyone.

## POINT TO PONDER:

When invited to provide our insights, we have to make sure to refrain from lecturing. We can provide advice in many ways, but if we want it to be accepted we should strike a gracious tone in our communication. If we reflect, we may see that the advice we have received and appreciated the most had been offered in a warm and kindly manner. Why blemish a beautiful relationship with an overly critical attitude if we can get so much further with a kind one?

# February 23

## GUIDING QUOTE:

*All human beings, by nature, desire to know.*

~ ARISTOTLE

## ACTION:

My quest for knowing keeps me proactive. I inquire without being intrusive, and I show interest without being nosy. I learn without becoming overly attached, and I teach without becoming overly confident.

## POINT TO PONDER:

There is a difference between wanting to know for self-improvement, and wanting to know to improve at the expense of others. Knowledge is a great asset, and we should not make it a liability.

One day Chuang Tzu and a friend were walking by a river. "Look at the fish swimming about," said Chuang Tzu. "They are really enjoying themselves." "You are not a fish," replied the friend, "so you can't truly know that they are enjoying themselves." "You are not me," said Chuang Tzu, "so how do you know that I do not know that the fish are enjoying themselves?"

*(Adopted from John Suler, "Zen Stories to Tell Your Neighbors")*

# February 24

## GUIDING QUOTE:
*An optimist is a person who sees a green light everywhere.*
*The pessimist sees only the red light. But the truly wise person is color-blind.*
~ ALBERT SCHWEITZER

## ACTION:

I work on my wisdom and apply color-blindness toward events as well as people. I see opportunities and take notice of warnings. I realize that there are multiple perspectives. I respect them all.

## POINT TO PONDER:

Acting color-blind is an interesting concept in today's world. It is wise to apply it in our approaches to others and to circumstances, so that we do not taint our perceptions with bias.

A traveler through the mountains came upon an elderly gentleman who was busy planting a tiny almond tree. Knowing that almond trees take many years to mature, he commented to the man, "It seems odd that a man of your advanced age would plant such a slow-growing tree!" The man replied, "I like to live my life based on two principles. One is that I will live forever. The other is that this is my last day."

# February 25

**GUIDING QUOTE:**

*What you are is what you have been,*
*and what you will be is what you do now.*

~ BUDDHA

**ACTION:**

As I take full responsibility of my past actions, I accept the way I am now. I am delighted that it is in my power to establish the person I want to become. I contemplate on this and determine my actions toward my future being.

**POINT TO PONDER:**

We write our own future through our actions. Doing nothing today will result in an empty tomorrow. If only we could carry this wonderful piece of wisdom with us all the time, we would probably be more cautious and conscious in our actions and words. But while we tend to forget, this is a beautiful moment to be reminded of our own immense power to create the person we want to be. Our future is very much in our own hands. Who do we want to be? Let us think about that and start working toward it now.

# February 26

**GUIDING QUOTE:**

*You can not prevent the birds of sorrow from flying over your head,
but you can prevent them from building a nest in your hair.*

~ CHINESE PROVERB

**ACTION:**

I prevent the issues that are troublesome in my life to overshadow my being. Despondency is not my nature. I do not dwell on mishaps. They are mere lessons from which I learn. After the lesson I move on, for I am not a harbor of despair, but a temple of joy.

**POINT TO PONDER:**

If you look around, you will see plenty of people who allow the birds of sorrow to build a nest in their hair. They encounter hardship, and then settle for their circumstances and give up. They land on a monotonous treadmill of duty fulfillment or even lethargy, forgetting to open their eyes for life. These people, too, are teachers to us; they show us a pathway best avoided. Life is a gift that was given to all of us. Free. Why waste it?

# February 27

**GUIDING QUOTE:**
*When you want to be honored by others,*
*you learn to honor them first.*
~ SATHYA SAI BABA

## ACTION:

I practice humility and do not let aspirations for superiority get the best of me. I honor without expectations and trust it will plant a positive seed in my relationships.

## POINT TO PONDER:

Radio 1 to Radio 2: "Please divert your course 15 degrees North to avoid a collision." Radio 2 to 1: "Recommend you divert *your* course 15 degrees South to avoid collision." Radio 1: "This is the captain of a Navy ship; I say again divert your course." Radio 2: "No. I say again, you divert *your* course." Radio 1: *"This is an aircraft carrier, the second largest ship in the national fleet! We are accompanied by three destroyers, three cruisers, and numerous support vessels. I demand that you change your course 15 degrees North, that's one-five degrees North, or counter measures will be undertaken to ensure the safety of this ship."* Radio 2: "We are a lighthouse; your call."

# February 28

## GUIDING QUOTE:

*When one door of happiness closes, another opens; often we look so long at the closed door that we do not see the one that has been opened for us.*

~ HELEN KELLER

## ACTION:

I stop looking at the door that is now closed. Why stare at the past if the future is so promising? Doors close for a reason. I honor that, and look for the one that opens. This new door provides an even more rewarding perspective. I am looking.

## POINT TO PONDER:

Even though we know that everything happens for a reason, we often get bitter when things happen to us. Being human, we keep thinking of the lost opportunities and forego precious chances by doing so. The sooner we can recuperate from a loss, the sooner we will see fortune in our new opportunities. While we do not have a program for our life, we have proof enough from those who went before us that everything happens for a reason.

# February 29

**GUIDING QUOTE:**

*Human action can be modified to some extent,
but human nature can not be changed.*

~ ABRAHAM LINCOLN

**ACTION:**

I ensure that my actions are geared toward increasing the good and decreasing the bad. I know that human nature is often described as selfish, shortsighted, greedy, and cruel, but the very implication of the word *humane* clears up a lot. I practice humaneness and trust that I instigate a positive change.

**POINT TO PONDER:**

The statement above can be seen from a positive or negative angle. However, regardless of one's perspectives of human nature, positive actions can be implemented. While we still struggle with wars, famine, oppression, hate, and destruction, we can decide upon changing our actions in a constructive direction, each one for ourselves.

March

# March 1

**GUIDING QUOTE:**

*Nothing is enough for the man to whom enough is too little.*

~ EPICURES

**ACTION:**

I am proactive: I realize my goals and refrain from excessive ambition that negatively affects my outlook on life. My blessings are enough. I am content.

**POINT TO PONDER:**

An old man was so poor that his young daughter, Akanke, suggested that he pawn her. With a sad heart the old father did. The pawnbroker, a greedy, jealous woman, had Akanke grind corn and pepper on the village grinding stone everyday, even on the night of the goblins, when no villager was out. When the goblin chief asked Akanke why she was out grinding that night, she explained her plight. The goblins took pity on her and gave Akanke and her father enough money to pay off their debt and live a decent life. The greedy, jealous pawnbroker then sent her only son to grind, hoping she would also get money this way. Instead, the goblins unmasked her intentions, took her son from her, as well as all her money. Her greed cost her everything.

# March 2

### GUIDING QUOTE:
*Man is free at the moment he wishes to be.*
~ VOLTAIRE

## ACTION:
My freedom is in my mind. I think my own thoughts, decide upon my goals, and have my own dreams. I choose my attitude toward the things that happen to me.

## POINT TO PONDER:
Freedom, like happiness, wealth, and peace, is a state that each of us defines for ourselves. Unfortunately, often we are all too happy to subordinate our freedom to the actions and decisions of others. Yet, even the slave can be freer than his owner. Our bodies do not set us free. Our wealth does not set us free. Our job, house, position, and status do not set us free. Our thoughts, however, can set us free. Freedom is a very personal perspective, as everyone perceives it differently. We are all free to count our blessings and know that they are many, because even our perceived misfortunes are blessings in disguise.

# *March 3*

## GUIDING QUOTE:

*Intellectual growth should commence at birth and cease only at death.*

~ ALBERT EINSTEIN

## ACTION:

I am a student of and for life. My teachers are all around me: occurrences, people, ideas, animals, and plants. Through my teachers I grow. For this I am grateful.

## POINT TO PONDER:

Opportunities for growth are all around us, in people, readings, experiences, and in the ways our minds interpret them. Whether we choose to increase our intellectual growth, or not, is entirely up to us. Emotional intelligence is a significant facet of intellectual growth that takes feelings into consideration along with our capacity for critical reasoning. For either emphasis of intellectual capacity, Einstein's statement makes perfect sense: we can experience the wonder of life as long as we continue learning.

# March 4

**GUIDING QUOTE:**

*Glory is like a circle in the water,*
*Which never ceaseth to enlarge itself,*
*Till by broad spreading it disperses to naught.*

~ WILLIAM SHAKESPEARE

**ACTION:**

I am grateful for the recognition I receive. Yet, I do not let it blind me. Everything passes, and splendor and failure are each other's mirror images. I hold no expectations related to others' opinions. I accept their rewards and their demerits.

**POINT TO PONDER:**

It is beautiful to be glorified, but it is wise to keep in mind that everything is impermanent. Our glory, like our misfortune, is just a moment in time that evaporates as soon as something or someone else comes along. We often think that glory will last forever. This is foolish and only leads to despair. It is wiser to continue exerting effort, even at the height of our eminence, because the seasons of life are like the seasons in a year, which all have their value.

# March 5

## GUIDING QUOTE:
*Toil to make yourself remarkable by some talent or other.*
~ SENECA

## ACTION:
I consider my talents and their purposefulness. How can I improve? How can I make my talents gratifying to myself and to others?

## POINT TO PONDER:
After winning many contests, a boastful champion archer challenged an old master who was renowned for his skills. The young man flawlessly hit a distant bull's eye, and then split that arrow with his second shot. "There," he said to the old man, "see if you can match that!" The master motioned the young archer to follow him up a mountain. When they reached a deep chasm spanned by a rather flimsy and shaky log, the old master stepped onto the middle of the perilous bridge, picked a far away target, drew his bow, and fired a clean, direct hit. "Now, you," he said, as he stepped back onto the safe ground. The young man was frozen with fear. "You have much skill with your bow," the master said, "but you have little skill with the mind that releases the shot."

# March 6

**GUIDING QUOTE:**

*A banker is a fellow who lends you his umbrella when the sun is shining, but wants it back the minute it begins to rain.*

~ MARK TWAIN

**ACTION:**

I do not rely on tokens of affection in good times. Instead, I work up strength for rainy days when all my supporters withdraw and go into hiding.

**POINT TO PONDER:**

On the sunny days we have to prepare for the rains that will undoubtedly come. We cannot be ready for every rainfall, but we can be open to learning and determined to revive and grow. Friends, colleagues, our entire society is programmed to embrace us when things are well, and let us down when they are not. Self-awareness helps us accept this ebb and flow gracefully. What we often fail to see is that the lack of support in hard times provides us with opportunities to increase in strength and to grow. We should be thankful to those who fail us when we need them most. They, too, are important teachers.

# *March 7*

**GUIDING QUOTE:**
*Do not go where the path may lead;*
*go instead where there is no path and leave a trail.*
~ RALPH WALDO EMERSON

**ACTION:**

Today, I outshine myself. I refrain from taking the easy road of followership. I become the difference I want to see in the world.

**POINT TO PONDER:**

Even though it is easy to follow the examples of others, it is better to use their actions as a source of inspiration to develop in our own way. There are infinite roads to explore, and there are countless approaches to explore those roads. If life has taught us anything, it is that, just when we think there is nothing new possible, another option appears. So why shouldn't we become the trendsetters of our day? We can create new paths at our work, in our industry, in our area of expertise, as a result of our knowledge, experience, and self-reflection. Our talents have been waiting too long to come out. Now is the time to bring them out.

# *March 8*

## GUIDING QUOTE:

*A smooth sea never made a skilled mariner.*

~ ENGLISH PROVERB

## ACTION:

I face my problems with courage and see them as opportunities to develop my skills. Hurdles inspire me to use my full dexterity as I rediscover my goals and the strength I have to reach them.

## POINT TO PONDER:

It isn't pleasant when complications surface, but in retrospect, every complication is an opportunity to enhance our creativity and make us more valuable. Besides, every challenge sharpens our awareness of the value of our goal. If there were no challenges, what would we have to contemplate on and teach to upcoming generations? We would take our achievements for granted and forget their value. A rough sea is no pleasant experience while it lasts, but it makes for great sailors.

# March 9

*Do not look where you fell, but where you slipped.*

~ AFRICAN PROVERB

## ACTION:

I review the causes of my failure or disappointment rather than become upset about the occurrence itself. Taking time to do so enlightens me about the real problem I need to address.

## POINT TO PONDER:

If we consider that we are ultimately responsible for what happens to us, we also need to realize that our actions from the past lead to many of the things we go through today. Sometimes the reasons behind our current problems are deeply buried and require intense contemplation for discovery. We may not be able to undo the issues that caused current pitfalls, but we can reflect and learn. We will only grow intellectually if we have the courage to face the causes of our dilemmas, rather than condemn their effects.

# March 10

## GUIDING QUOTE:
*Be not ashamed of mistakes and thus make them crimes.*

~ CONFUCIUS

## ACTION:

I am a happy high-achiever. I do my best in all my activities, and am not embarrassed by my mistakes. Mistakes are steps on the ladder toward future success.

## POINT TO PONDER:

We all make mistakes sometimes. The trick is to refrain from making the same mistake all the time, and that boils down again to the crucial art of life: learning. It is good to remember that behind every flawless appearance there hides a person with as many or more flaws than you. Those who are officially labeled to be fools are often not the biggest fools in town. People are masters in disguising their faults, but that does not mean that they do not have them. This should be a point of encouragement for all of us to continue working toward our goals.

# March 11

## Guiding Quote:

*Fear less; hope more. Eat less; chew more. Whine less; breathe more. Talk less; say more. Love more, and all good things will be yours.*

~ SWEDISH PROVERB

## Action:

I minimize my words and maximize my acts. I listen, maintain a positive outlook, and support those who need my service to my best abilities.

## Point to Ponder:

The above proverb's direct statement requires little explanation. It simply confronts us with the basics of living wisely. This paradigm shift from negative to positive, from shallow to deep, from destructive to constructive, and from useless to useful, can be a great way to show our family, friends, colleagues, customers, students, teachers, and all those we encounter what the essence of interconnectedness is. Yet, even when we know these basics, we need some reminding now and then to stay the course. Especially the call to love more can never be overstated in our world. Love instigates love.

# March 12

## GUIDING QUOTE:

*A bird does not sing because it has an answer.*
*It sings because it has a song.*

~ CHINESE PROVERB

## ACTION:

I sing my song in the best way I know, because I want to contribute and make my life and the lives of those around me more pleasant.

## POINT TO PONDER:

Perspectives are often distorted by expectations. Like a bird, we may not always have a solution, but that doesn't mean that we cannot perform. And because we know how easy it is for others to expect different things from us than we are willing or able to give, we should not make the same mistake. It speaks of greatness to take things as they are and not as we want them to be.

# *March 13*

### GUIDING QUOTE:

*When the character of a man is not clear to you, look at his friends.*

~ JAPANESE PROVERB

### ACTION:

Others judge me by the friends I have. I am therefore careful in choosing my friends. I select my friends on the basis of their character, trustworthiness, and reliability.

### POINT TO PONDER:

A man was walking with his dog when he realized that they were both dead. They came upon an estate with pearly gates. "Come in," said the gatekeeper. "Where are we?" "This is heaven," said the guard. "Can my friend come?" "Sorry, no dogs." The man remembered the devotion of his dog, then turned away and resumed his walk. They arrived at a farm, where a man was standing. "Come in," said the guard. "What about my friend?" "He is welcome too." "Where are we?" "This is heaven," said the guard. "Heaven? They told me that at the other place." "That was hell," said the guard. "We do not mind them using our name. That way they harbor all those who disregard their true friends for material things."

# March 14

### GUIDING QUOTE:
*Where love reigns the impossible may be attained.*
~ INDIAN PROVERB

## ACTION:

I give more love and care to others than they expect, because I know how much I could achieve if I were loved and cared for more than I expected.

## POINT TO PONDER:

Susan became blind through a medical error. After her initial anger and despair, she started moving on, supported by her husband Mark, an Air Force officer who loved and cared for her deeply. When Susan had to return to work, she was overcome with fear. But Mark drove her back and forth for weeks, until he realized that this would not work over the long term. He suggested that she start taking the bus again, like before. Susan was devastated, but Mark rode along for two weeks, until she was comfortable enough to do it alone. One day, a bus driver told Susan, "You're a lucky woman!" Upon her puzzled look, he explained that a man in military uniform watched her from a distance daily, making sure she made the bus safely, then blew a kiss and saluted her.

*(Modified from a story by Neutral Singh)*

# March 15

## GUIDING QUOTE:

*If a person shaves you with a razor,
do not shave him with broken glass.*

~ SURINAMESE PROVERB

## ACTION:

I treat others well. If someone goes out of his or her way to serve me or make me feel comfortable, I return the favor. In doing so, I create a climate of warmth and goodwill for the future.

## POINT TO PONDER:

Reciprocity is an important way to show other people that you appreciate them. Status and appearance should not matter. When others treat us with dignity, we should treat them with even more admiration in return. Even when they do not treat us as well as they could, we should set a good example and treat them better. The universe is an interconnected whole. What goes around comes around.

# March 16

## GUIDING QUOTE:

*The more you know, the less you need.*

~ ABORIGINAL AUSTRALIAN PROVERB

## ACTION:

I open myself for wisdom. I do not let my priorities get out of order, but am content at each stage of my journey.

## POINT TO PONDER:

A management consultant asked a fisherman why he caught such a small catch of fish with his fishing boat. The fisherman explained that the small catch sufficiently met his family's needs. The consultant asked, "What do you do with the rest of your time?" "I sleep late, fish, play with my children, rest under a tree, visit friends, and sing songs. I have a full and happy life." The consultant ventured, "I have an MBA from Harvard and I can help you. You should fish longer every day. Then you sell the extra fish, buy more boats until you have a large fleet, and open your own plant." "And then?" asked the fisherman. "Then you can start selling shares in your company and make millions! After that you'll be able to retire, sleep in late every day, play with your children, rest under a tree, visit friends, and sing songs."

# March 17

## ACTION:

No one is to blame for my shortcomings, and now, I convert my shortcomings to strengths. I can create opportunities by working toward them. I can dance.

## POINT TO PONDER:

In a tollbooth in San Francisco, there was a man dancing to loud music. One driver asked him what he was doing. The man said he was having a party. When the driver pointed to the other quiet booths, the man said, "They're not invited!" Months later, the intrigued driver passed the music-filled tollbooth again. The dancing operator smiled and said, "Still having a party!" The driver asked, "What about the other sixteen operators?" "They die every morning when they come to work, and resurrect every evening to go home." "Why are *you* having such a good time?" asked the driver. "I'm going to be a dancer someday, and my bosses are paying for my training. I have a corner office with a great view. I'm having a party!" Dancing through life is up to us.

# March 18

## GUIDING QUOTE:
*He who divides and shares, always takes the best part.*
~ CHILEAN PROVERB

## ACTION:
I realize that unfairness is part of human nature. Yet, I am fair in all my decisions. Where I can, I make a positive change, no matter how small.

## POINT TO PONDER:
One wonders if those who engage in taking the best part when they are in a position of power have a sense of guilt from their unfair practices, or if they consider it to be only reasonable? If the above statement holds true, we cannot speak of equality. Fortunately, we can change some things we do not agree with at our own level. We may not be able to change a social system, but we can change ourselves and set an example of fairness.

# *March 19*

*One who does not look ahead remains behind.*

~ BRAZILIAN PROVERB

## ACTION:

I review where I currently am, and where I am going with my life. I set out a plan toward this future goal, and examine what I need to do to make it happen. I do not waste time, and I enjoy the journey toward my future.

## POINT TO PONDER:

Remaining stationary is equal to regress in our work environment. It is important for us to continue developing ourselves, learn inside and outside our immediate area of expertise, and find new ways to stay active. Creativity is one of the wonderful gifts of human beings. Creativity can be nurtured so that it grows. It is only when we become passive that our creativity diminishes. Getting ahead has everything to do with being creative. We should remember that.

# March 20

**GUIDING QUOTE:**
*Don't cry because it's over. Smile because it happened.*
~ DR. SEUSS

**ACTION:**

I take the things as they come. If a relationship, event, or experience ends, I remain grateful for the fact that it once was. If I cry and stare at a door that got closed, I lose the opportunity to find the new one that has opened.

**POINT TO PONDER:**

It takes greatness to take things as they happen. However, it is the only real way for us if we want to continue enjoying life. Life is a continuous cycle of beginnings and endings. Losing something we thought would remain forever is not easy, but dwelling on the past is the most foolish thing we can do. It delays future happiness, and therefore deters understanding as to why something had to happen this way. The sooner we move on, the sooner the understanding comes.

# *March 21*

*Your task is not to seek for love, but merely to seek and find all the barriers within yourself that you have built against it.*

~ RUMI

## ACTION:

From here onward, I let go of the reservations I have against love. I turn inward and look for the answers to my fears. Where do they come from? How can I turn them into courage? Knowing that the answers lie within, I think on that.

## POINT TO PONDER:

In the course of our lives we get confronted with disappointments that cause us to become cautious when others offer their love. We become suspicious and try to analyze the motives behind the warmth they offer. Thus, we alienate important people from us. However, there are ways to responsibly break down the barriers and open up ourselves again for love. These ways start with examining our reactions to others, detecting the reasons, and removing the barriers.

# *March 22*

## GUIDING QUOTE:

*A happy life consists in tranquility of mind.*

~ CICERO

## ACTION:

I do not allow any agitation to overwhelm me and upset my stability. I remain focused, fulfill my duties as efficiently as I can, and keep my mind calm.

## POINT TO PONDER:

Through the ages, many wise people have made statements similar to the above one. Many successful people have proven the legitimacy of these statements. Our circumstances can be highly unfavorable, but depending on our mind-set, we will be able to withstand them. A tranquil mind can weather even the harshest circumstances, while a troubled, scattered mind cannot stand even a slight wind shift. Practice tranquility of mind.

# March 23

**GUIDING QUOTE:**

*Do you want a collection of brilliant minds or a brilliant collection of minds?*

~ R. MEREDITH BELBIN

**ACTION:**

I respect my group members, and I understand the advantages and pitfalls of group engagement. I belong to many groups, official and unofficial, through membership or by nature. I respect them and remain alert.

**POINT TO PONDER:**

Teamwork can be gratifying in various forms. When the Navy jet piloted by Charles Plumb was shot down on his seventy-sixth mission, he parachuted down. He was captured and imprisoned, but survived and now shares his story with the world. One day, a man approached him and told him that he was the one who had packed Plumb's parachute. Plumb realized how much he was indebted to this unknown team member. He thanked him for saving his life. Teams have great advantages, if you remain wary of the free riders and bad apples.

# March 24

## GUIDING QUOTE:

*A stupid man's report of what a clever man says
can never be accurate, because he unconsciously translates
what he hears into something he can understand.*

~ BERTRAND RUSSELL

## ACTION:

I realize that modes of thought set in motion by a person with good intentions can become adulterated when advanced by less conscious individuals. Therefore, I distance myself from thoughtless followership, and engage in mindful self-leadership.

## POINT TO PONDER:

When the spiritual teacher and his disciples began their evening meditation, the cat that lived in the monastery made such noise that it distracted them. So the teacher ordered that the cat be tied up during the evening practice. Years after the teacher had died, the cat continued to be tied up during the meditation session. And when the cat eventually died, another cat was brought to the monastery and tied up. Centuries later, learned descendants of the spiritual teacher wrote scholarly treatises on the religious significance of tying up a cat for meditation practice.

*(Adopted from John Suler, "Zen Stories to Tell Your Neighbors")*

# March 25

### GUIDING QUOTE:
*Remember that there is nothing stable in human affairs;*
*therefore avoid undue elation in prosperity, or undue depression in adversity.*
~ SOCRATES

### ACTION:
I accept my circumstances with peace of mind, knowing that nothing is stable. I am not envious of those who live in affluence, nor am I disheartened by my own lack of fortune in some areas. I am blessed in my own way.

### POINT TO PONDER:
People are usually drawn to those who seem to be affluent, because they want to be associated with the standards of success as formulated by society. However, material affluence does not guarantee happiness, and material modesty is no sign of misery. Rise above mediocre perspectives and start seeing things in their genuine light. Material issues are not representative of who and what we really are.

# March 26

## Guiding Quote:

*A man is rich in proportion to the number of things he can afford to let alone.*
~ Henry David Thoreau

## Action:

Need and greed do not drive my actions. I can do without a lot of the things I see, read, or hear about. I am OK where I am.

## Point to Ponder:

A dog held a juicy bone in his jaws as he crossed a bridge over a creek. When he looked down into the water, he saw another dog below with what appeared to be a bigger, juicier bone. He jumped into the creek to snatch the bigger bone, letting go of his own. He quickly learned of course that the bigger bone was just a reflection, and so he ended up with nothing.

*(Adopted from Aesop's Fables)*

# March 27

**GUIDING QUOTE:**

*What is uttered from the heart alone, will win the hearts of others to your own.*
~ JOHANN WOLFGANG VON GOETHE

**ACTION:**

I speak from the heart, yet also in a manner that is not hurtful to those I share my honesty with. I can be honest without hurting other people's feelings. I do not do unto others what I would not want done unto me.

**POINT TO PONDER:**

Being straightforward is not synonymous with being mean. It attests to sensitivity and respect if we can state our genuine opinion in a gentle and respectful way. The receiver of such beautiful candidness will be more willing to listen and take note of your comments than if they were expressed in a harsh and hurtful manner. The universe is interconnected. Kind comments bear a pleasant atmosphere for all of us.

# March 28

## GUIDING QUOTE:

*I have never met a man so ignorant that
I couldn't learn something from him.*

~ GALILEO GALILEI

## ACTION:

Everybody is my teacher. Even those individuals whom everyone considers foolish have something to teach me. Life is precious. I learn from my teachers.

## POINT TO PONDER:

Ignorance is the root of much of the suffering in the world, yet there is something to be learned from it. We can learn from those who act out of ignorance, and from those who refrain from acting out of ignorance; from those close to us, and from those detached; from the wealthy, the famous, and the revered, but also from the drunks, the drugged, and the homeless; they all carry important lessons for us if we are open and willing to learn from them. The way we learn and grow is a curriculum unique to each of us.

# March 29

## GUIDING QUOTE:

*No man likes to have his intelligence or good faith questioned, especially if he has doubts about himself.*

~ HENRY ADAMS

## ACTION:

I speak my mind with care, and do not get upset when others have different opinions or when they get upset about my view. I respect them.

## POINT TO PONDER:

Every response and every behavior, has roots that we could understand if we stopped long enough to regard them. Since we usually do not, we often stand surprised at others' aggression when they find their opinions questioned. Yet, we should understand that those who get upset easily when confronted with different views may be vulnerable or insecure. Perhaps we would have responded the same way if we were in their shoes. We should therefore question kindly, and accept the responses gracefully.

# March 30

## GUIDING QUOTE:

*The world is a tragedy to those who feel, but a comedy to those who think.*
~ HORACE WALPOLE

## ACTION:

I feel *and* think, so I am influenced by emotions based on both senses. I prioritize neither, and remain healthily detached. I love without being devastated, and I reason without being offended.

## POINT TO PONDER:

The chief would give a feast and ask each guest to bring one calabash of wine. One man wanted to attend very badly but had no wine to bring. His wife suggested that he buy the wine, but he thought, "If hundreds of people pour their wine into the chief's pot, one calabash of water can't spoil it." The day of the feast came. Each man poured the contents of his calabash into the chief's large pot. The man poured his water. When all the guests had arrived, the chief ordered to fill everyone's cup with wine. At the chief's signal, all the guests put their cups to their lips and were surprised to taste…water. Each guest had thought that his calabash of water would not spoil the pot of wine.

*(Adopted from a Nigerian folktale)*

# *March 31*

### GUIDING QUOTE:
*Men occasionally stumble over the truth, but most of them pick themselves up and hurry off as if nothing ever happened.*
~ SIR WINSTON CHURCHILL

## ACTION:

Hypocrisy is not a part of my actions. Neither is untruthfulness. I realize that societies are rarely founded upon finding and telling the truth. Many people are scared of it. But how can I otherwise face myself?

## POINT TO PONDER:

Truth is an interesting subject that may not be the same for all of us. We see things based on who we are. But when we find our own truth, we should not ignore it. That would be the worst example of self-deception. Facing the truth takes courage, but it makes character as well. Truth is not always beautiful, but it should be preferred at any time. Avoiding the truth is not only an insult to the intelligence of others, but it damages our own sense of purpose in life as well.

*April*

# April 1

*Before we set our hearts too much upon anything,*
*let us examine how happy those are who already possess it.*

~ FRANCOIS DE LA ROCHEFOUCAULD

## ACTION:

I examine my desires. Who owns the things I want? Is it within my competency to want them? Do I need them? Whom am I hurting by taking them? I curtail my desires as much as possible.

## POINT TO PONDER:

The world is full of temptation. There are beautiful things that we can buy, and those that we can get. Yet, what we often overlook is that much of the anger, hatred, and pain in the world is caused by people taking what belongs to others. Whether at the personal level or in greater context, desire often causes damage to one or more parties. The pain starts within the one who acquires the desire, and spreads further from there. Is the fulfillment of every desire worth all the pain and effort it demands?

# *April 2*

*The cause is hidden. The effect is visible to all.*

~ OVID

**ACTION:**

I consider the causes of my current life situation. What got me here, and where do I wish to move to from here? When I encounter negative or mean behavior, I consider that this is an effect of something I may not be aware of. That is how I can understand better and forgive more easily.

**POINT TO PONDER:**

Everything we see, feel, or hear is an effect of something else. The wisdom we generate over time illuminates the eternal cycle of cause and effect. Because this cycle has been in existence forever, each cause is an effect of a previous cause, and each effect a cause of a previous effect. It is easy to judge an act we see or a statement we hear. It takes compassion and self-transcendence to realize that there is always an underlying cause. We should therefore regard everything around us in context, so that we may attain a higher level of contentment.

# April 3

*Youth is happy because it has the capacity to see beauty.*
*Anyone who keeps the ability to see beauty never grows old.*
~ FRANZ KAFKA

## ACTION:

As my life advances, seeing the beauty in everything becomes a greater art. Disappointments, failures, or encounters with hardship may have clouded my views and made it harder to recognize the magnificence of all I see, but why wait until I can no longer see before I realize that everything is beautiful in its own way? Today, I look for the beauty in everything.

## POINT TO PONDER:

Beauty resides in everything—in nature, animals and plants, in the things we create, and in those we do not. Beauty inspires a sense of awe, and a sense of awe inspires the realization of the wonder that is life. Seeing beauty allows us to live fully. Failing to see beauty slowly weakens the essence of our life. Seeing and acknowledging beauty is a spirit-lifting experience for both the source and the observer.

# April 4

### GUIDING QUOTE:
*Those who wish to appear wise among fools, among the wise seem foolish.*
~ QUINTILIAN

## ACTION:
I behave in a way that is true to who and what I am. I have no reason to be arrogant, as I am continuously learning. Arrogance is the foolishness in which pseudo-wizards engage.

## POINT TO PONDER:
A man wanted his four sons to learn not to judge things too quickly. He sent each of them to look at a pear tree that was a great distance away. The first son went in winter, the second in spring, the third in summer, and the youngest son in fall. When they had all gone and returned, he called them together to describe what they had seen. The first son claimed that the tree was ugly, bent, and twisted. The second son said it was green and full of promise. The third said it was laden with blossoms and beautiful, and the last said it was full of life and fulfillment. The man then explained to his sons that they were all right, and that you cannot judge a tree, or a person, by only one season.

# April 5

*I'm lazy. But it's the lazy people who invented the wheel and the bicycle because they didn't like walking or carrying things.*

~ Lech Wałęsa

## Action:

I engage in constructive laziness. I try to find convenient ways to do my work optimally without affecting the quality. In this way I sharpen my mind.

## Point to Ponder:

There is a crucial difference between constructive and destructive laziness. Constructive laziness leads to the invention of devices to make a task easier, like Wałęsa indicated above. Destructive laziness leads to a rusty brain, a sluggish spirit, and self-pity. The only laziness we should allow ourselves is the first. In general, the word lazy has a negative connotation. That is because most people considered lazy practice the destructive type of laziness: unproductiveness. Yet, if you use your mind to improve the quality of your life, you are no failure.

# April 6

**GUIDING QUOTE:**

*The whole secret of life is to be interested in one thing profoundly and in a thousand things well.*

~ HORACE WALPOLE

**ACTION:**

I contemplate on my major source of interest in life. By recognizing this source, I am able to explore the roads toward mastering it. Today is a good day for self-exploration.

**POINT TO PONDER:**

The most contented people are those who have determined their calling. Why? Because they know which way they are going. Some discover their main interest early on, while others need to contemplate a while longer. More importantly, our main interest may change as our life advances. Yet, as long as we keep ourselves focused on the question, what do we want to be remembered for, we are making progress. The only regress would be if we were to give up and take a position on the treadmill of thoughtless performance like so many others.

# April 7

## GUIDING QUOTE:
*I will master something, then the creativity will come.*
~ JAPANESE PROVERB

## ACTION:

I consider my purpose, and then work toward its realization. The more I focus, the more skilled I become. The more skilled I become, the more creative I am. The more creative I am, the better I can serve those who enjoy my work.

## POINT TO PONDER:

In the past 50 years the Japanese have utterly lived the perspective of mastery first and creation next. They learned how to make devices, and were first ridiculed for the lack of quality. But as time went on, skills improved. Today, Japanese audio-visual, transport, and robotic technologies lead the world. It's a process that takes time, but ultimately is rewarded tremendously. We should learn from that. If we want to be great painters, we must first need to learn how to paint. If we want to be great educators, we must first become educated.

# April 8

## GUIDING QUOTE:

*Discretion is being able to raise your eyebrow instead of your voice.*

~ ANONYMOUS

## ACTION:

Everyone has his own perspectives and truth. Even if I turn out to be right, I might behold a friend and maintain everyone's dignity by refraining from raising my voice. Attitude speaks louder than words. I am discrete.

## POINT TO PONDER:

When hearing a perspective that we do not agree with, our first impulse may be to dispute it, and the more forceful the other party is, the more forceful we become. This drains energy from all parties involved. It works this way in work-related discussions, gossip, and any other conversations that raise topics we feel strongly about. Keeping quiet is always the wisest strategy. Why should we enter disputes with others, even if we think they are wrong? As far as we know now, we could be as much in the wrong as those we rebut.

# April 9

## GUIDING QUOTE:

*The moment you have in your heart this extraordinary thing called love and feel the depth, the delight, the ecstasy of it, you will discover that for you the world is transformed.*

~ JIDDHU KRISHNAMURTI

## ACTION:

I share my affection with others and help them experience the greatness of giving without expecting, granting without taking, and loving without setting conditions.

## POINT TO PONDER:

A young taxi driver had to pick up a customer. He honked several times, but no one came. Most drivers would have left, but he walked up to the apartment and rang the bell. An old lady with a suitcase opened. Behind her the furniture was covered with sheets. The driver asked where she needed to be, and she gave an address, but requested to drive through town. He told her that was not the shortest way. She said, "I'm in no hurry. I'm on my way to a hospice. I do not have any family or time left." Then he turned off his meter and drove her around for two hours before taking her to her final address. He didn't charge. Love is great.

# April 10

**GUIDING QUOTE:**

*Discontent is the first necessity of progress.*

~ THOMAS A. EDISON

**ACTION:**

I bring about change when I feel that something around me or within me is not providing me the satisfaction or gratification I envision. Discontent, used as a forerunner to everything new and improved, is constructive.

**POINT TO PONDER:**

Discontentment is nothing more than the lowest side of contentment. It is up to us to raise our contentment level, and we can do that through thorough evaluation of our circumstances. Nothing changes by just sitting around and waiting. The initiatives are for us to take, and the results will follow. So what are the areas in which we are discontented? How can we change them? Today is a great day to examine this.

# April 11

### GUIDING QUOTE:
*The good and the wise lead quiet lives.*
~ EURIPIDES

## ACTION:
The world is as good a place as I make it. I am selective about the tasks I engage in. I use my time sufficiently, and prevent matters from landing in the crisis mode.

## POINT TO PONDER:
Why continue to be victimized by a hectic and unsatisfying lifestyle that only elevates our blood pressure, elicits anxiety, and robs us of those precious moments with loved ones? Quietude is a precious gift that too many of us unfortunately forego in our attempts to gain fame and fortune. Even though history has proven time and again that everything is temporary, we continue to make that mistake. Yet, it is not too late to become wise and engage in a less stressful, quieter lifestyle in order to enjoy every moment to an infinitely higher degree.

# April 12

## GUIDING QUOTE:

*Write the bad things that are done to you in sand,*
*but write the good things that happen to you on a piece of marble.*

~ ARAB PROVERB

## ACTION:

I choose to remember every positive deed done unto me. My mind is filled with positive thoughts. Those positive thoughts smooth the path for my loved ones and myself.

## POINT TO PONDER:

Two friends were walking in the desert. They got into an argument and one friend slapped the other in the face. The slapped friend didn't say anything but wrote in the sand, "Today my best friend slapped me in the face." After a while, they found an oasis and decided to take a bath. But the slapped friend was caught in the mire and started drowning. The other helped her. After she recovered, she wrote on a stone, "Today my best friend saved my life." The friend asked her, "Why did you write in sand when I slapped you and on stone when I saved you?" She replied, "The sand note will be blown away by the winds of forgiveness. The one in stone can never be erased."

# April 13

*Listen or thy tongue will keep thee deaf.*

~ NATIVE AMERICAN PROVERB

**ACTION:**

I listen to the people and things around me. I concentrate on what they say through words, gestures, and other expressions. I only speak when necessary. This is how I learn.

**POINT TO PONDER:**

In many Western societies people are taught that they should speak up. They subsequently engage in superfluous talking, even if they do not really have anything important to say. This is unfortunate, because while we talk we do not learn. When we think we can overpower others by the sound and rapidity of our talk, we only deceive ourselves. People quickly learn who we are, what we are, and what we think, and they can easily determine where and how to undermine us. Listening is a virtue that brings us wisdom.

# April 14

## GUIDING QUOTE:

*Everyone is kneaded out of the same dough but not baked in the same oven.*

~ YIDDISH PROVERB

## ACTION:

I respect the people I meet, whether they are old, young, tall, small, Black, White, able-bodied, or challenged in any way. The world is a beautiful place, thanks to their presence.

## POINT TO PONDER:

Humanity is a beautiful and invaluable amalgamation of diverse cultures, perspectives, and habits. While some of the habits from members of other groups may be hard to understand, we should continue to revere them. Just as their ways seem strange to us, ours seem strange to them too. There is something to be learned from everyone. This is, more than ever before, the time to learn from one another. The ovens in which we were baked are now more accessible than ever before. Let us continue to enjoy and respect our unique differences.

# April 15

## GUIDING QUOTE:

*Do not judge by appearances; a rich heart may be under a poor coat.*

~ SCOTTISH PROVERB

## ACTION:

I do my best wherever I am. I respect everyone, regardless of his or her looks. I understand that there is more to life than looks. Goodness comes in many shapes.

## POINT TO PONDER:

A poor farmer once heard a boy crying. The boy had wandered into a swamp nearby and was rapidly sinking. The farmer quickly tied himself to a tree and waded into the drifting sand. In what seemed to become the final struggle for both, the farmer finally managed to bring the boy and himself to safety. He took the boy home, and his wife cleaned him up and washed his clothes. Then they took the boy home. The next day a large car stopped in front of the farmer's dwelling. Out came a wealthy man, the father of the boy. He offered to reward the farmer, but the farmer said that he saw his act as a moral duty. Then the rich man saw the farmer's son, and insisted on paying his education. Both boys later became important men in history.

# April 16

## GUIDING QUOTE:
*We never know the worth of water 'til the well is dry.*

~ ENGLISH PROVERB

## ACTION:

I value even the simplest things and do not take anything for granted. Everything, even the simplest act, item, or person, can be gone the next moment. I am grateful while I can enjoy them.

## POINT TO PONDER:

Everything passes. Good things and bad things, happy moments and sad moments. Even the things and people we consider a given in our lives will one day move on. Even our life will cease to continue as it is. It is therefore of no use to hold onto things or people, nor to take them for granted. Coming to terms with the relativity and impermanence of things is an important understanding on our way to increased consciousness.

# April 17

*If you are patient in one moment of anger,
you will escape a hundred days of sorrow.*

~ CHINESE PROVERB

**ACTION:**

I think before I speak, because I want to refrain from regretting my thoughtlessness. I maintain patience and save others and myself from humiliation and grief.

**POINT TO PONDER:**

We often say unforgivable things in moments of anger. It is so easy to let go of our rage, especially when we think someone deserves it. At work, at home, and even among friends there are enough moments in which we can get upset about things others do incorrectly. Yet, the art of living lies in those moments when our impulses direct us to do one thing, and our deeper, more responsible inner-self tells us something else. Usually the impulsive voice is much louder and more clearly present. Our deeper, more responsible inner-self remains calm and tries to keep us from engaging in irresponsible behavior. Training ourselves to listen to the soft rather than the loud voice can ensure graceful existence.

# April 18

## GUIDING QUOTE:
*When spider webs unite they can tie up a lion.*
~ AFRICAN PROVERB

## ACTION:
I am not able to do everything alone. Some things require team play. With the right team members and a good plan, we can all achieve much more.

## POINT TO PONDER:
Brother Lion, Sana goat, her children, and Anansi, the legendary spider, lived in the same house. One day, Lion decided that he wanted the house for himself. He chased out Sana, her children, and Anansi, who ran for their lives, but got stranded at a large lake. Sana started crying as Lion rapidly approached. Anansi quickly turned Sana and her children to stones and threw them across the river. As soon as they touched the other side, they turned into goats again and ran into the forest to hide. Meanwhile, Lion got very close. But Anansi threw a long, silver line across the river. He slid across his own silver spider thread and got away. Lion pawed the thread down and got entangled in it.

*(Adopted from a Nigerian folktale)*

Moral: Teamwork and efficiency outperform greed and brutal force.

# April 19

*The road to a friend's house is never long.*

~ DANISH PROVERB

**ACTION:**

I know the difference between friends and acquaintances. My friends are special to me. I treat them as such, and they do the same in return. We support one another.

**POINT TO PONDER:**

While we should be true and available to friends, we should be cautious about labeling others as such. There are many acquaintances, but not that many friends. A friend is rare and establishes him- or herself in hard times. A friend is like a root on the tree that we are. Acquaintances are like branches and leaves. They come and go. Yet, even when we have not been able yet to determine whether someone is a friend or an acquaintance, we should still give as much as possible without expecting anything in return.

# *April 20*

## Guiding Quote:

*Pain is inevitable; suffering is optional.*

~ Hindu spiritual saying

## Action:

I may not be able to escape all the hardships, disappointments, and aches that life has in store for me, but I can determine my attitude toward them. I choose not to suffer long, but perceive each challenge as a lesson through which I can learn and grow stronger.

## Point to Ponder:

It is easy to blame circumstances or other people for the things that are going wrong in our lives. Many people do that. It shifts the responsibility for the quality of their life to others. But how realistic is that? Suffering is, ultimately, a very personal experience, a determination we all make for ourselves. While some people suffer a long time over something that went wrong, others distill their lessons and move on. Which course of action do you choose?

# April 21

**GUIDING QUOTE:**

*It is easy to be brave from a safe distance.*

~ AESOP

**ACTION:**

I speak my mind cautiously and politely whether near or far from others. I listen and refrain from giving unasked directions. I speak when asked.

**POINT TO PONDER:**

It is amazing how brave people become when they do not have to act upon a problem. We can often see it in war movies, where the decision makers, often thousands of miles away from the problem, radio directions through that are simply inexecutable on location. The interesting thing is, if we were to place these decision makers in the midst of the problem, their bold decisiveness might be nowhere to be found. We should therefore be careful in implementing inconsiderate counsel of people who talk easier than they walk.

# April 22

*If you don't like something, change it.*
*If you can't change it, change your attitude. Don't complain.*

~ MAYA ANGELOU

**ACTION:**

I work on my attitude in situations that I cannot change. I do not dwell on a sense of discontentment. For any uneasy feeling, I find the source and do something about it.

**POINT TO PONDER:**

An ass, belonging to an herb seller who gave him too little food and too much work, requested another master of Jupiter. Jupiter warned him that he might repent his request, and had the ass sold to a tile maker. The loads were heavier and the work harder, and again the ass requested for a change of environment. Jupiter warned that this would be the last change, and had the ass sold to a tanner. This time, not only was the work heavier, but the situation merciless. The ass realized that this owner surpassed the hardships of the previous ones, and would even use him in death by tanning his hide to sell. Moral: He who finds discontentment in one place is not likely to find happiness in another.

*(Adopted from Aesop's Fables)*

# April 23

### GUIDING QUOTE:

*The roots of education are bitter, but the fruit is sweet.*

~ ARISTOTLE

## ACTION:

I work diligently toward my goals, so that it feels great when I reach them. Hard work is never easy, lessons to be learned never simple, hurdles to surmount never insignificant. But once I have made progress, I can rightfully be proud of myself.

## POINT TO PONDER:

Everything that happens to us is a lesson that we have to learn. Education, formal and informal, is all around. We all have many lessons to learn; how quickly or slowly we learn depends on us. The sooner we decide to learn, the faster the progress, and the sooner the pain from an experience subsides. The more we reject learning, the more frequently the same lesson will occur in different forms. What would an achievement mean anyway without any effort? How can we learn if everything is handed to us on a silver platter? How can we pass any lessons on to others if we do not learn?

# April 24

*Mystery creates wonder and wonder is the basis of man's desire to understand.*

~ NEIL ARMSTRONG

## ACTION:

Today, I break through the boundaries of my limitations. I enlarge my horizons by exposing myself to different areas of knowledge. I pick up a different book, talk to a different person, or take a different route to work. I do something out of the ordinary to stir up my sense of wonder. This is my first attempt at understanding more.

## POINT TO PONDER:

We have an innate inclination to stick to familiar territory and avoid the unknown. As human beings, we prefer to minimize risk. Yet, by staying in the comfort zone, we also prevent ourselves from being exposed to new things and expanding our perspectives. Doing something new on a regular basis can help us break through this pattern and invite the next breakthrough.

# April 25

*People see God every day, they just don't recognize Him.*
~ PEARL BAILEY

## ACTION:

I nurture the awareness that there is something sacred and wonderful in everyone and everything I meet. I realize that the good things and the seemingly bad things that happen to me are lessons that I need to learn on my way toward growth. I do my best to learn them and see the higher purpose of it all.

## POINT TO PONDER:

We often look for major and rare occurrences to find confirmation of the presence of a higher being. In our quest to find this confirmation in larger-than-life events, we can miss many beautiful manifestations throughout our day. It is so easy to look back at the end of the day and shrug it off as a "normal" one, simply because there were no major highs or lows. But the smiles, kind words, and the little blessings, such as arriving home safely and being able to have a meal, are too easily forgotten.

# April 26

## GUIDING QUOTE:

*Before anything else, preparation is the key to success.*

~ ALEXANDER GRAHAM BELL

## ACTION:

I make an extra effort today to be the best person I can be. I may not be able to prepare for everything, but I can ensure that I am the best I can be under all circumstances. I make this day a better one for everyone I meet.

## POINT TO PONDER:

A group of engineers successfully tested airplane windshields on their suitability of withstanding bird-strikes by developing a powerful gun, with which they shot dead chickens onto the airplane windshields. This success was widely revered in many articles. Engineers elsewhere read the article and tried the process with the same gun, but with no success. Their windshields were smashed to pieces by the chickens. When they wrote to the successful team about their mishaps, the response was brief: "You need to defrost the chickens first!" Preparation makes all the difference.

# April 27

**GUIDING QUOTE:**

*Little by little, through patience and repeated effort,
the mind will become stilled in the Self.*

~ BHAGAVAD-GITA

**ACTION:**

My mind is often like a restless child, quickly bored and easily distracted. Today, I think on ways to still my mind in the self. I choose my preferred way, whether yoga, meditation, or just silent contemplation. Today, I make a start toward stilling the mind.

**POINT TO PONDER:**

Everything requires repeated practice before we can attain mastery. Mindfulness is a particularly challenging state to attain in our hectic world full of surprises, while mindlessness is so easy to fall prey to. Just when we think we have achieved a point of stillness, another challenge surfaces that disrupts the stillness of the mind and switches us back to scatter-brain mode once more. Yet, practice in silencing the mind is possible, and the roads are many. We can start with quiet breathing exercises, focusing on our breaths, every time a little longer.

# *April 28*

**ACTION:**

I create opportunities to apply my skills, knowledge, and intelligence. I pay attention to my skills and review areas that I have neglected. I am open to opportunities.

**POINT TO PONDER:**

A teacher faced her class and told her students she liked them all equally. This was a lie, because little Teddy always looked messy and performed badly. The teacher even took delight in failing him for his bad work. But then she reviewed the notes from Ted's past teachers. She learned that in previous grades he had been a bright and happy student until his mom died. The teacher felt embarrassed and decided to help Teddy. She stopped teaching courses and started teaching children. Years after the class, Teddy kept writing her that she was the best teacher he ever had. He became a medical doctor, and at his wedding, the teacher took the honorary place of Ted's mom. She had added opportunity to Ted's ability in a crucial time.

# *April 29*

**GUIDING QUOTE:**

*Those who are most slow in making a promise are*
*the most faithful in the performance of it.*
~ JEAN JACQUES ROUSSEAU

**ACTION:**

I make my promises with caution, as I keep in mind how hurtful it can be for
others when I do not keep them, even if against my will. By being true to my
word toward others, I contribute my share of positive energy to the universe.

**POINT TO PONDER:**

Many of us have been hurt and became cynical from all the promises we heard
others make to us, and from finding out that they did not keep them. We should
reflect on that and refrain from hurting others in the same way by making hollow
promises. Whether at work, home, or elsewhere, our promises should be sacred.
The promises we make, but even more the degree to which we are known to keep
them, help establish our reputation. Moreover, they help us create our self-image.
That alone is reason enough to keep our promises as consistently as we can.

# April 30

## GUIDING QUOTE:

*Start by doing what is necessary, then do what is possible,
and suddenly you are doing the impossible.*

~ SAINT FRANCIS OF ASSISI

## ACTION:

I can transcend my limitations by stretching my boundaries, one step at the time. I can do this in my actions toward myself and others. This is how I will reach greater heights than ever before.

## POINT TO PONDER:

Lethargy is a serious problem. If we want to realize our dreams, we will have to look for opportunities, and oftentimes we will have to create them ourselves. Only when we engage in focused actions toward reaching our potential will we increase our chances of success. By playing it safe and dwelling only on the possible, we gradually take steps backward, until even the possible will have become impossible.

# May

# May 1

### GUIDING QUOTE:

*It is a man's own mind, not his enemy or foe, that lures him to evil ways.*

~ BUDDHA

### ACTION:

I can achieve my goals in positive or negative ways. While the evil road may often seem shorter and easier, I deliberately seek the positive way. I am the one who controls my mind, and not the other way around.

### POINT TO PONDER:

We are all born with a Buddha mind. Yet, as life progresses, we can be influenced by people, processes, and problems, and develop habits that stand in the way of our enlightened perception. Our mind gets clouded and cluttered. Nevertheless, we have a choice. We can tune into our intuition and our perceptions, and examine which direction is the proper one to take. Ultimately, that is our own responsibility. And the enlightened mind is right here. Within. It is our responsibility to restore it. No one else's.

# May 2

*The fact that I can plant a seed and it becomes a flower,*
*share a bit of knowledge and it becomes another's, smile at someone and*
*receive a smile in return, are to me continual spiritual exercises.*

~ LEO BUSCAGLIA

**ACTION:**

I work toward establishing the effect I want to cause. I enrich the quality of my life by investing in positive aspects in order to increase the chance of positive returns.

**POINT TO PONDER:**

Outcomes are not always what we anticipate them to be. But that should not be a reason to refrain from dealing a positive hand where and when we can. A smile doesn't cost anything, nor does a word of support, nor a listening ear when one needs it. The spiritual outcome of some of our actions is not immediately visible and sensible, but it does appear. Unwaveringly.

# May 3

**GUIDING QUOTE:**

*Cowards die many times before their deaths;*
*The valiant never taste of death but once.*

~ WILLIAM SHAKESPEARE

## ACTION:

I may not be able to change the things that happen to me, but I can change my attitude toward them. I see every loss as a gateway toward improvement, and every closed door as an indication toward greater directions.

## POINT TO PONDER:

A master of the tea ceremony in old Japan once accidentally slighted a soldier. He quickly apologized, but the soldier demanded a settlement in a sword duel. The tea master, having no experience with swords, asked his friend, a swordsman, for advice. The swordsman knew about the concentration and tranquility of the tea master. He told him, "Tomorrow, when you duel the soldier, hold your weapon above your head and face your opponent with just as much concentration and tranquility as when you serve tea. The tea master did so, and the soldier was captured by the tea master's tranquility. He lowered his sword, apologized, and left.

# May 4

## GUIDING QUOTE:

*I have reached the conclusion, a bit late perhaps, that speeches should be short.*

~ FIDEL CASTRO

## ACTION:

I communicate effectively, whether in official or unofficial settings. I keep matters interesting, understandable, and pleasant for all parties involved. I show compassion for my audience and keep it short and sweet.

## POINT TO PONDER:

There is a story about Abraham Lincoln, who wrote a very long letter to a friend and apologized that he had no time to be brief. It takes preparation to be concise and to the point. The higher we climb the career ladder, the more we think that we should impress others with the extent of our speeches, the forcefulness of our presence, and the elaboration of our memo's and letters. We make the mistake of thinking that more is meaningful, but later we learn that less is more. It's better to have your audience yearn for more than wonder if you're ever going to stop.

# May 5

**GUIDING QUOTE:**

*Darkness cannot drive out darkness; only light can do that.*
*Hate cannot drive out hate; only love can do that.*

~ MARTIN LUTHER KING, JR.

**ACTION:**

I do not respond to the mean practices of others with mean practices. There is no gratification in doing that. I remain kind and supportive, even to those who give me a hard time in my work.

**POINT TO PONDER:**

As a young dark-skinned lawyer, Gandhi was thrown off the train in South Africa. He spent the night in the cold with bitter anger about such discrimination. This night, he explained later, became the enlightening turnaround in his life. He understood after deep contemplation that hate would not be eradicated by hate. Gandhi started the non-violence movement, and achieved more than he would have ever achieved with hateful force. Growth lies in showing the way, whether the other party understands or not. Let us try to be the light.

# May 6

**GUIDING QUOTE:**
*Surrender is faith that the power of love can accomplish
anything...even when you can not foresee the outcome.*
~ DEEPAK CHOPRA

**ACTION:**

I surrender to the insecurity and constant changes of life. I refrain from anger
and spite. Instead, I spread my love, forgive, and realize that everything passes.

**POINT TO PONDER:**

One day, King Solomon asked his brightest minister, Benaiah, to bring him a
special ring. It should be a ring with magic powers, which could make a happy
man sad and a sad man happy. Benaiah set out to find this ring and traveled for
months, yet, in vain. A day before the deadline, Benaiah, now desperate, wandered through the poorest part of town. He met a simple merchant and asked
him if he knew of a ring that could make a happy person forget his joy and a sad
one forget his sorrow. The man took a ring and engraved a simple scirpt inside.
The next day, the King called for Benaiah, who handed Solomon the ring. The
king immediately realized that all his wisdom and wealth were fleeting things.

# May 7

## GUIDING QUOTE:

*Who has confidence in himself will gain the confidence of others.*

~ LEIB LAZAROW

## ACTION:

Am I doing what I want to do? If not, I change my direction. If so, I stand behind my actions and go for my goals. I am the leader of my life, and my success depends on my self-confidence.

## POINT TO PONDER:

Upon completing a highly dangerous tightrope walk over Niagara Falls in appalling wind and rain, The Great Zumbrati was met by an enthusiastic supporter who urged him to make a return trip, this time pushing a wheelbarrow, which the spectator had thoughtfully brought along. The Great Zumbrati was reluctant, given the terrible conditions, but the supporter pressed him. "You can do it—I know you can," he urged. "You really believe I can do it?" asked Zumbrati. "Yes—definitely—you can do it." the supporter gushed. "OK," said Zumbrati, "Get in the wheelbarrow…."

# May 8

**GUIDING QUOTE:**

*Nothing in life is to be feared; it is only to be understood.*
*Now is the time to understand more, so that we may fear less.*

~ MARIE CURIE

**ACTION:**

I look deeper into daily occurrences, and do not take matters personally. This is how I get rid of a defensive demeanor, and become more open to offerings and remarks of others without distrusting them beforehand.

**POINT TO PONDER:**

It is so easy to become paranoid about matters of life. There seem to be so many selfish people in the world who only care about their own well-being. This particularly seems to be the case in workplaces. Yet, living in constant fear paralyzes and withholds personal and professional progress. We should therefore seek to understand people and processes around us, so that we may grasp the bigger scope of their actions.

# May 9

### GUIDING QUOTE:
*It is the enemy who can truly teach us to practice the virtues of compassion and tolerance.*

~ THE DALAI LAMA

**ACTION:**

I respect those who challenge me, because their sharp criticism teaches me to be better prepared in everything I do.

**POINT TO PONDER:**

"How many enemies boundless as the sky might I destroy," wrote the Buddhist poet, Santideva. "Yet when the thought of hatred is abolished, all enemies are destroyed." "How," asked the Buddha, "will hatred ever leave anyone who forever thinks: 'He abused me; he hit me; he lied to me; he robbed me'? There is an enduring law: hatred never ceases through hatred; hatred only ceases through love." Everyone appears in our life for a reason. We usually like the friends and dislike the foes. But friends only try to make us feel good about ourselves. Our enemies make us alert of our weaknesses and force us to become stronger, brighter, wiser, and more resilient. Our enemies are therefore valuable teachers.

# May 10

### GUIDING QUOTE:
*Better to remain silent and be thought a fool than to speak out and remove all doubt.*

~ ABRAHAM LINCOLN

## ACTION:
I think twice before I speak. I consider the fact that too many people speak before their turn, or speak for the sake of speaking. I refrain from that behavior.

## POINT TO PONDER:
It is amazing to hear how much nonsense people voice when they speak without thinking. Unconsidered words can be useless at best and harmful at worst to others, as well as to the one uttering them. In many societies, especially the Western ones, we are taught to let our voices be heard. We thereby think too much about being heard and too little about the meaning of our words. We ingnore the fact that what we say tells others a lot about who we are. It is good to think about that here and now, and adjust our speaking habits accordingly.

# *May 11*

### GUIDING QUOTE:
*Boredom: the desire for desires.*
~ LEO TOLSTOY

### ACTION:
I keep my body, mind, and spirit active in as positive a way I can. I realize that boredom can create room for malicious thoughts and desires. I therefore choose to remain engaged.

### POINT TO PONDER:
If idleness is the devil's playground, boredom is his home. People who are bored can think of the most destructive things, usually geared toward others who have good intentions with their lives. By giving in to their boredom, they can ruin other people's well-being. Boredom is also a fertile ground for depression, which can lead to self-destruction. Fortunately, we have minds, so even in the most restricted environments we can keep a part of ourselves active.

# May 12

## GUIDING QUOTE:

*It is the dissimilarities and inequalities among men which give rise to the notion of honor; as such differences become less, it grows feeble; and when they disappear, it will vanish too.*

~ ALEXIS DE TOCQUEVILLE

## ACTION:

I strive to earn respect and honor from my fellow humans by focusing on my talents and skills, and on those aspects that improve well-being for all: kindness, helpfulness, understanding, empathy, and love.

## POINT TO PONDER:

In our quest to get ahead of everyone else, basic values become insignificant. While de Tocqueville is right about the decline of dissimilarities and inequalities, especially in this era of ubiquitous connection through technological devices, he may have overlooked the fact that different reasons will contribute today in earning honor and respect. Returning to inter-human respect and acts of compassion sets an example for others. There are still many great ways to distinguish ourselves.

# May 13

**GUIDING QUOTE:**

*Principles for the Development of a Complete Mind: Study the science of art. Study the art of science. Develop your senses—especially learn how to see. Realize that everything connects to everything else.*

~ LEONARDO DAVINCI

**ACTION:**

With the realization that everything connects to everything else, I show proper respect and kindness to every living being I encounter today. We are all part of a bigger whole, so they are part of me as much as I am part of them. I embrace life and all living.

**POINT TO PONDER:**

It is such a waste of our precious mind power to use it selectively. While our mind provides the skills to determine our way ahead, it can also help us to see our connection with everything. Unfortunately, we have become numb to this awareness, but we can awaken it again to gain greater happiness for ourselves and benefit all to whom and to which we are connected.

# May 14

**GUIDING QUOTE:**

*If we could see the miracle of a single flower
clearly, our whole life would change.*

~ BUDDHA

**ACTION:**

There is infinite beauty in everything that nature provides. Yet, I seldom pay attention to the miracles growing around me. Today I devote some special time to pay attention to nature's gifts. I admire the flowers and trees, and count my blessings for being able to do so.

**POINT TO PONDER:**

It is too easy to take things for granted in our hectic daily lives. We step on grass, not realizing how blessed we are to have grass. We stand in the shade of trees, ignoring how blessed we are to have trees. We see flowers and walk by them or pluck them, failing to realize the works of art that they are. If we care to do so, our awareness of the greatness of existence will increase.

# May 15

*Once I dreamed I was a butterfly, and now I no longer know whether I am Chuang Tzu, who dreamed I was a butterfly, or whether I am a butterfly dreaming that I am Chuang Tzu.*

~ CHUANG TZU

## ACTION:

My self-perception is an image that may be deceptive. I created it, but it may not be the same image that others see in me, nor even what I really am. Today, I contemplate on the difference in perceptions, and make sure to be the best person I can be toward everyone I meet.

## POINT TO PONDER:

Appearances come and go. The way we look today is not how we will look five years from now. So why are we so hung up on appearances? Why do we judge others on theirs? We may not even be what we think we are. We may not look like the reflections we see. We transform continuously, even if we do not see it. Yet, we often think that we are better than animals, plants, or people from other places. How silly.

# May 16

**GUIDING QUOTE:**
*He who knows others is wise.*
*He who knows himself is enlightened.*
~ LAO TZU

**ACTION:**

I have been focusing on knowing others all my life, but how well do I know myself? Have I ever contemplated the things I would really like to do? Am I truly engaging in what I like, or am I going through the motions, postponing self-reflections and their outcomes for an eternal tomorrow? Today, I contemplate on that.

**POINT TO PONDER:**

We often hear that life is too short. Yet, many of us allow ourselves to remain stuck in circumstances and activities that we dread. We are so busy marching in line with what peers, colleagues, bosses, and even strangers want from us, that we do not wonder what we want from ourselves. The good life starts with knowing what you appreciate and then engaging in it. It makes every day so much more worthwhile.

# May 17

### GUIDING QUOTE:

*When you have only two pennies left in the world,
buy a loaf of bread with one, and a lily with the other.*

~ CHINESE PROVERB

## ACTION:

Balance is what keeps me content. Living this life of constant pressure sometimes drives me to make irrational decisions. Today, I take a moment to think, and I focus on balance in my actions.

## POINT TO PONDER:

We often fail to realize that we are being lived by the requirements of our daily life: our jobs, our families, and the organizations we are members of—they all demand our time and dictate our actions. Oftentimes, these dictates steer us too much in one direction and too little in others. We lose our balance. But there should be a time for everything: duty and leisure, activity and rest, nourishment and beauty.

# May 18

**ACTION:**

Today, I keep in mind that all that glitters is not always gold. People at work often get into prominent positions because they know how to sell themselves. To prevent myself from being just another small thing made large by advertising, I let my actions speak louder than my words—not only today, but from now on.

**POINT TO PONDER:**

It seems as if our entire life is programmed by sales. We are all in sales. There is nothing wrong with that per se, unless we over-sell ourselves, which is what many people do. They blow up and polish their resume and their self-promotion, and hide their flaws until they have achieved their goals. While some may look upon this as an outstanding skill and an achievement unto itself, it is a dangerous deception that may lead to severe disappointments for others as well as ourselves.

# *May 19*

## GUIDING QUOTE:
*It is not enough to have a good mind;*
*the main thing is to use it well.*

~ RENÉ DESCARTES

## ACTION:

I am smart and intelligent, but I also make my share of mistakes. Many of these can be attributed to mindlessness: speaking before I think, being stubborn, or simply going through the motions. Today, I observe my mind. I observe my decisions. I pay attention to my thoughts.

## POINT TO PONDER:

There are many intelligent people who are unhappy with their jobs and their lives in general, because they do not use their mind optimally and creatively. They have built invisible walls around their thought processes and do not dare to transcend those walls. Because of that, they settle for mediocrity, and bring up the excuse that they have no choice or time to do something about it. Using the mind could make a world of difference in the quality of one's life.

# May 20

**GUIDING QUOTE:**

*Ambition is so powerful a passion in the human breast,
that however high we reach we are never satisfied.*

~ NICCOLO MACHIAVELLI

**ACTION:**

I am grateful for the ambition that got me here, but I remain aware that ambition can lead to avarice.

**POINT TO PONDER:**

A dissatisfied stonecutter passed a rich merchant's house. He wished he were the merchant, and became him. But a high official passed by, carried in a sedan chair by soldiers. He wished he were the official and became him. It was hot in the chair. He looked at the bright sun and wished he were the sun. He became the sun. But a large cloud moved before him. He wished he were the cloud, and became the cloud. Soon the cloud was pushed away by the wind. He wished he were the wind, and became the wind. He blew everything away but a huge rock. He wished he were the rock, and became the rock. Then, he heard the sound of a hammer and felt himself changing. What could be stronger than a rock? He looked down and saw a stonecutter.

# May 21

## Guiding Quote:

*It is not necessary to change. Survival is not mandatory.*

~ W. Edwards Deming

## Action:

If I do not change, I will not survive. I cannot hold on to old habits, because they are obsolete. I cannot cling to old lessons, because they do not matter anymore. Today, I apply the changes that I have postponed for so long.

## Point to Ponder:

A student went to his meditation teacher and said, "My meditation is horrible! I feel distracted, my legs ache, and I'm constantly falling asleep!" "It will pass," the teacher said. A week later, the student came back to his teacher. "My meditation is wonderful! I feel so aware, so peaceful, so alive! It's just wonderful!" "It will pass," the teacher replied. Progress is only possible when we become the change.

# May 22

*We think too small. Like the frog at the bottom of the well.*
*He thinks the sky is only as big as the top of the well.*
*If he surfaced, he would have an entirely different view.*

~ MAO TSE TUNG

## ACTION:

I seek to enlarge my horizons. I examine my self-imposed boundaries. I evaluate if I am heading toward my full potential, or if I have allowed the boundaries of my direct environment to restrain my views.

## POINT TO PONDER:

Without realizing it, many of us allow our direct environment, particularly our jobs, to dictate the magnitude of our thinking. We all talk about thinking outside the box, but very few of us walk that talk. Yet, it is when we dare to surface and face the whole world as our potential area of operation, that the blinders start fading, and the horizon starts expanding. Our sky is not necessarily the limit.

# May 23

## GUIDING QUOTE:

*There is nothing like returning to a place that remains unchanged to find the ways in which you yourself have altered.*

~ NELSON MANDELA

## ACTION:

I change all the time. I am continuously influenced by new places, people, readings, viewings, and experiences. No longer do I hold on to the thought that I remain unchanged. Today is a new day for more change, leading to more growth.

## POINT TO PONDER:

Those of us who have revisited old places that used to be familiar to us realize very well what Mandela means with his statement. We change. Our eyes see the world differently today than they did some years ago. We look differently upon the things that happened to us. Old pains and disappointments become appreciated lessons; old glories become cherished memories. But we see them in a different perspective today. We have moved on.

# May 24

## Guiding Quote:

*The miracle is not to fly in the air, nor to walk on the water, but to walk on the earth.*

~ Chinese Proverb

## Action:

The things that seem so easy are not as easy as they seem. There are many challenges in my life, and I face them, interpret them, and resolve them to my best abilities, starting today!

## Point to Ponder:

We revere the great inventions of humankind, but we take our own skills for granted. Having these skills is only part of the blessings we enjoy. Using our skills for the well-being of ourselves and as large a group of other living beings as possible, that is the true art of living. We can go through life without mercy, care, or compassion, but such is a life wasted. The gift of life is vested in giving, not in taking.

# May 25

## Guiding Quote:

*Doubt is uncomfortable; certainty is ridiculous.*

~ Voltaire

## Action:

I consider the fact that there is no certainty in anything. Not in my job, not in having my loved ones around me, not even in my own life. I therefore cherish them and show my appreciation today.

## Point to Ponder:

There are different levels of doubt, and when our doubt is minimized, we tend to think that we have achieved certainty. However, no such thing exists. Getting used to the idea that nothing is certain may help us understand our past disappointments and our future failures. Life is unpredictable, which is why it is so scary to the weak, yet so enticing to the strong among us.

# May 26

**GUIDING QUOTE:**

*It is an old maxim of mine that when you have excluded the impossible, whatever remains, however improbable, must be the truth.*

~ SIR ARTHUR CONAN DOYLE

**ACTION:**

I remember that trust is a beautiful virtue that should be applied within responsible bounds. I trust my co-workers, but I am not blind to the truth, even if it is inconvenient.

**POINT TO PONDER:**

In our care and love for those around us, we often allow ourselves to become blind to the truth. However, we should realize that even the closest and most beloved person could go wrong. While finding out the truth is not always pleasant, it can prevent the compilation of ignored offenses that lead to a huge, irreparable dilemma. The faces of the truth are not always pretty, but they are still true.

# May 27

## GUIDING QUOTE:

*Charisma becomes the undoing of leaders. It makes them inflexible, convinced of their own infallibility, unable to change.*

~ PETER DRUCKER

## ACTION:

I am watchful of my ego, and prevent it from growing to unhealthy proportions, which leads to delusional ideas. I open up myself to change and look, listen, and learn.

## POINT TO PONDER:

Many leaders who start out very humble and compassionate lose their bearings as their popularity increases. It takes strong legs to carry the wealth of reverence, especially when one is charismatic and outspoken, and is used to everyone listening. People who are used to being listened to often think that they are great and that no one can teach them anything. They fail to listen, and this becomes their demise.

# May 28

## GUIDING QUOTE:
*I have not failed. I've just found 10,000 ways that don't work.*
~ THOMAS ALVA EDISON

## ACTION:
If my plans do not work out right today, I do not adopt a sense of failure, but take to heart the lessons enclosed in what has happened, and move on.

## POINT TO PONDER:
Our joy or distress in life depends on our attitude. Everybody experiences setbacks now and then. These setbacks occur for a reason: they teach us humility and prickle our creativity. Resilience and perseverance form the recipe to achieve ultimate success after initial disappointment. The brightest people who ever lived, like Edison, make many mistakes before they hit their target. Why should we give up after a few setbacks?

# May 29

## GUIDING QUOTE:

*Nothing is perfect. Life is messy. Relationships are complex.*
*Outcomes are uncertain. People are irrational.*

~ HUGH MACKAY

## ACTION:

I do my best at everything, but when I am done, I am done. I do not dwell infinitely on my work, because there is a time for focusing and a time for moving on.

## POINT TO PONDER:

A preacher managed his garden with great perfection. One day, when he was expecting important guests, he raked all the leaves in his garden, cut the grass, and made sure everything was absolutely perfect. An old Zen master who lived next door was watching. The teacher sighed and said, "Isn't this perfect?" "Indeed," said the old man, "but there's one thing missing." "Missing? What?" asked the preacher, looking around. "Help me over this wall, and I will correct it." The preacher helped the old man over the wall. The man walked to the tree in the middle of the garden and shook it, so that leaves fell all over the garden floor. "There," said the old man, "Now you can help me back to my place."

# May 30

## GUIDING QUOTE:
*The truest characters of ignorance are vanity, and pride and arrogance.*
~ SAMUEL BUTLER

## ACTION:

I listen to what others have to say. I remember the virtue of humility, and do not let arrogance stand in my way.

## POINT TO PONDER:

A young officer, who was on his way to attend a lecture by a famous wise man, stepped from a train. He called for a porter to carry his bag, but an older man, who also arrived with the train, asked him, "Can't you carry your bag yourself and save the money?" The young officer replied, "It is not in keeping with my dignity to carry my bag. I am an educated person." The older man replied, "The hallmark of education is humility, not pride. I shall carry your bag if it is below your standard." When the young officer attended the lecture, he found out that his "porter" was the distinguished speaker of the evening. Ashamed, he reflected, "What is his education and what is mine? I am like a glow worm before the sun."
*(Modified from a story by Sathya Sai Baba)*

# May 31

**GUIDING QUOTE:**
*Those who don't know how to weep with their whole heart,*
*don't know how to laugh either.*
~ GOLDA MEIR

**ACTION:**

Whatever I do today, I do it with my entire being. If this is a sad day, I contemplate on my reasons for being sad, and make sure they are justified. If this is a happy day, I am happy with my entire being. I go all the way, wherever my path takes me.

**POINT TO PONDER:**

We are emotional beings. Unfortunately, some of us have become too good at masking our feelings. This is difficult for those we have dealings with, because they cannot measure our feelings. It is also harmful to us, as we have placed a lid over our emotional well, and this can lead to disastrous outcomes. People who show no emotions under any circumstance are hard to trust and hard to please. We should be aware of these effects.

June

# June 1

### GUIDING QUOTE:

*Though we travel the world over to find the beautiful,*
*we must carry it with us or we find it not.*

~ RALPH WALDO EMERSON

## ACTION:

The world outside is a reflection of myself. I see beauty and love in everything. I look for the positive in the things and people I meet, and value them for that.

## POINT TO PONDER:

A Zen master lived the simplest kind of life in a little hut at the foot of a mountain. One evening, while he was away, a thief sneaked into the hut only to find there was nothing in it to steal. The Zen master returned and found him. "You have come a long way to visit me," he told the prowler, "and you should not return empty-handed. Please take my clothes as a gift." The thief was bewildered, but he took the clothes and ran away. The master sat naked, watching the moon. "Poor fellow," he mused, "I wish I could give him this beautiful moon."

*(Adopted from John Suler, "Zen Stories to Tell Your Neighbors")*

# June 2

## GUIDING QUOTE:

*It is often merely for an excuse that we say things are impossible.*

~ FRANCOIS DE LA ROCHEFOUCAULD

## ACTION:

My life is proof of the fact that nothing is impossible. I reached this point, so why not reach for further heights? I believe in myself and in those around me, and maintain a positive view on the possibilities of our future.

## POINT TO PONDER:

What would people from the Middle Ages say if they could see our cars, airplanes, or the Internet? If they knew how quickly we travel from one end of the world to another, and how instantly we communicate with people thousands of miles apart? History has taught us that no dream is unachievable. Yet, there are always people who will tell us that our ideas are impossible. We should realize that those people are merely fearful or discouraged. But why should we share their fear?

# June 3

### GUIDING QUOTE:
*When you're through changing, you're through.*
~ BRUCE BARTON

### ACTION:
I am not averse toward altering my ways if I find they do not serve me. I am not afraid to change my plans if I realize they do not work. Change is a sign of living. I am alive.

### POINT TO PONDER:
Some people insist that they do not change. Those people probably do not have mirrors, and they surely do not observe their thought processes or feelings regularly. Change is nothing new. It has always been a part of life. Everything that lives, changes—all the time, even though we do not see it readily. Change is a fascinating and enriching process. It ensures the spice of life. So why reject change? Why reject the notion of changing continuously? If we do so, we are like ostriches sticking our heads in the sand.

# June 4

*If you don't make mistakes, you're not working on hard enough problems. And that's a big mistake.*

~ FRANK WILCZEK

**ACTION:**

My mistakes are my steps toward improvement. I am not embarrassed if I make a mistake, because I realize that mistakes are part of my growth, an indication that I am doing something that I can learn from.

**POINT TO PONDER:**

Imagine a world with no mistakes. How arrogant would we be? And how much would we learn? The greatest lessons come from failures and mistakes. The greatest inventions came about after huge and repeated mistakes. Making mistakes indicates something wonderful: learning. Why stay in an eternal comfort zone and dull our brains? We owe it to existence to be the best we can be, and we cannot be that if we always stay on the safe side.

# June 5

### GUIDING QUOTE:
*If indeed you must be candid, be candid beautifully.*
~ KAHLIL GIBRAN

### ACTION:
I am forthcoming, yet not hurtful. I am honest, yet kind. I respect others and leave them their dignity, regardless of the things I have to say to them.

### POINT TO PONDER:
A sharp tongue has never made anyone happy. It creates hurt and anger, so why should we maintain such a thing? Everything can be said in different ways. We do not have to sugarcoat the truth to still say it in a way that is void of meanness. Brought into the perspective of work, a nice example: The chicken and the pig agree to co-host a barnyard breakfast. The chicken suggests that they serve bacon and eggs. The pig replies, "For you that means involvement. For me it's total commitment."

*(Adopted from Ken Blanchard and Sheldon Bowles,*
*"Gung Ho: Turn on the People in Any Organization")*

# June 6

## GUIDING QUOTE:

*Every moment is a golden one for him who has the vision to recognize it as such.*

~ HENRY MILLER

## ACTION:

I look for the opportunity in every moment—the one in which I receive a compliment, the one in which I receive a reprimand, and the one in which nothing is said. I realize that all these moments help me to grow.

## POINT TO PONDER:

History is full of stories of people who saw opportunities where others only saw doom and gloom. Those who had the vision wrote history and are revered today for their contributions. It takes an eager and positive attitude, combined with a creative mind, to see opportunities. We shouldn't expect to see them all the time, because we are human beings, so we have some days that are more inspired than others. Yet, if we can regularly attempt to see the big picture of our actions and detect the lessons in our encounters, opportunities will reveal themselves at the least expected moments.

# June 7

### GUIDING QUOTE:
*Love makes time pass; time makes love pass.*
~ FRENCH PROVERB

## ACTION:
I help make my surroundings pleasant, so my work does not feel like drudgery, but rather like a constructive way of utilizing my time while contributing to a rewarding result. I cherish my connections, knowing that everything, including myself, will be gone tomorrow.

## POINT TO PONDER:
There are two deep messages enclosed in this simple phrase: in an environment of love, time is of no importance and passes by quickly. On the other hand, a stretched amount of time makes everything pass, even love. We come and go like leaves on a tree. Today we're young and green, tomorrow, dried up and faded. Senses of affection ripen, just like everything else. Nothing ever stays the same. Not even love.

# June 8

**GUIDING QUOTE:**

*With true friends...even water drunk together is sweet enough.*

~ CHINESE PROVERB

**ACTION:**

In the presence of my family, friends, and colleagues, my life is good. Mutual care and support are priceless.

**POINT TO PONDER:**

Dola and Babi were longtime friends. They even got married to two brothers. Dola sowed a cola nut, but as it grew, animals were eating the leaves. Babi brought her a bottomless pot to place around the tree. The tree grew and brought forth many fruits. Dola became wealthy, but Babi got jealous and demanded her pot back. Dola cried, but nothing helped. The judge decided that Babi should get her pot, so the tree was cut. Soon Babi got a baby girl. Dola brought her a nice brass ring for the baby's neck. When the girl was ten, Dola demanded her ring back. Babi cried, but nothing helped. The judge decided that Dola should get her ring, so the girl would have to be beheaded. But Dola told Babi that she would not pay bad for bad. The girl was saved, and they remained friends.

*(Adopted from a Nigerian folktale)*

# June 9

## GUIDING QUOTE:
*Those who wish to sing, always find a song.*

~ SWEDISH PROVERB

## ACTION:

I am focused. I am blessed. I am fortunate to know where I am heading. Even if I do not have a long-term plan, I am convinced that I am on the right track. I keep walking in the right direction.

## POINT TO PONDER:

The foundation of a successful life lies in the will to achieve. An achiever always seeks a source of achievement, and then runs with it. Having a purpose is like having your own special song. You sing it, and you feel gratified. You feel that you are valuable, even if others do not recognize it yet. It will be a matter of time before they do. The beauty and strength of your song will attract the right ears at the right time.

# June 10

*Habits are first cobwebs, then cables.*

~ SPANISH PROVERB

## ACTION:

I examine my habits. I review their influence on others and myself, and consider the advantages and disadvantages of having them. I decide which ones I need to nurture and which ones will have to go, and start working on making that happen.

## POINT TO PONDER:

Not all habits are bad. There are just as many good habits as there are bad ones. Yet, we can enhance the quality of our life by examining our habits regularly and ensuring that we do not become their victim. Sometimes our habits can stall us from growth, make us ill, or alienate us from dear ones. Those habits need to be released, even though they may have become strong cables that are hard to cut.

# June 11

**GUIDING QUOTE:**
*Every path has its puddle.*
~ ENGLISH PROVERB

**ACTION:**

The setbacks that I face today will not get me down. Setbacks are merely puddles on my path: challenges that allow me to think creatively. I will therefore even be grateful for my puddles today, as they help me grow.

**POINT TO PONDER:**

Two monks were traveling down a muddy road. Around the bend they met a lovely girl in a silk kimono and sash, unable to cross the intersection. "Come on, girl," said one of the monks. Lifting her in his arms, he carried her over the mud. The other monk did not speak again until that night when they reached a lodging temple. Then he burst out, "We monks can't be near females, especially not young and lovely ones. It is dangerous. Why did you do that?" "I left the girl there," said the first monk. "Are you still carrying her?" If we did not encounter any puddles in our lives, we would be weak and dull-minded. The challenges that we encounter sharpen our vision and challenge our sense of creativity.

# June 12

*If you want happiness for an hour—take a nap. If you want happiness for a day—go fishing. If you want happiness for a month— get married. If you want happiness for a year—inherit a fortune. If you want happiness for a lifetime—help someone else.*

~ CHINESE PROVERB

## ACTION:

The most beautiful moments of my life are the moments I can serve. I make an effort to help others. I keep my eyes and ears open, and help at least one person in need. By doing that, I am sending goodness into the universe.

## POINT TO PONDER:

Two people are lost in the desert. They are dying from hunger and thirst. Finally, they come to a high wall. On the other side they can hear the sound of a waterfall and birds singing. Above, they can see the branches of a lush tree extending over the top of the wall. Its fruit look delicious. One of them manages to climb over the wall and disappears down the other side. The other, instead, returns to the desert to help other lost travelers find their way to the oasis.

*(Adopted from "101 Zen Stories")*

# June 13

## GUIDING QUOTE:

*A friend is one to whom one can pour out all the contents of one's heart, chaff and grain together, knowing that the gentlest of hands will take and sift it, keeping what is worth keeping, and, with the breath of kindness, blow the rest away.*

~ ARAB PROVERB

## ACTION:

I think on my real friends who showed me that I can trust them. I thank them for that. At the same time, I make sure that I am a real friend. Loving, forgiving, and trustworthy.

## POINT TO PONDER:

It takes great character and much love to accept a person in his or her entirety, with perfections and flaws, blessings and mishaps. Finding such a friend is hard, but not impossible. Being such a friend is not easy either, but it enhances the chances of finding a real friend in return. Friendship can be found everywhere—at home, in social places, and at work. Let us be the best friends we can be—everywhere.

# June 14

**GUIDING QUOTE:**

*However long the night, the dawn will break.*

~ AFRICAN PROVERB

**ACTION:**

I am happy today, because the sun is near. I may not have seen the signs yet, but I know improvement of my situation will be here soon. With this belief I make the best of my day.

**POINT TO PONDER:**

There are some things in life that are inevitable: the dawn of a new day after every night, for instance, and the impermanence of everything, regardless of how good or bad. While we laugh about our fortune or cry about our pain, we should realize that they, too, are temporary. This understanding can help us remain down to earth, and not lose our heads when times are great, nor despair too deeply when times are rough. Everything passes.

# June 15

### GUIDING QUOTE:
*The old pipe gives the sweetest smoke.*
~ IRISH PROVERB

**ACTION:**

I respect the people and processes that have been around for a long time. While I will still embrace change, I keep in mind that the old ways and people had to be there in order to ignite new ones. Their expertise and dedication are admirable. I am thankful.

**POINT TO PONDER:**

It is easy to fall prey to the attraction of a comfort zone. Established ways have, after all, already proven themselves, and the chance that they will go wrong is narrow—at least for the moment. But even the sweetest smoke ends one day, so we have to be on alert in creating alternatives that are as good, or better, than the established, familiar way. It is good to know that we can count on the love and affection of people and things that have been around for the longest time. Yet, we should also realize that one day we will have to let them go.

# June 16

**Guiding Quote:**
*As if you could kill time without injuring eternity.*
~ Henry David Thoreau

**Action:**

I use my time wisely, and engage in activities that enhance well-being for others and myself. I do not waste my time on things that have little meaning. I lay the foundation for a meaningful future!

**Point to Ponder:**

Every action we take contributes to the overall quality of life. Not just our life, but also the lives of many others, even those we do not know. We should therefore grant our actions their import, making sure they are constructive and meaningful. This will not only provide us with a better sense of gratification, but also serve as a foundation for a rewarding life and a solid contribution to the progress of life on earth. Killing is never good, so killing time is as unacceptable as any other form of killing. We should think on that.

# June 17

## GUIDING QUOTE:

*All our progress is an unfolding, like a vegetable bud. You have first an instinct, then an opinion, then a knowledge as the plant has root, bud, and fruit. Trust the instinct to the end, though you can render no reason.*

~ RALPH WALDO EMERSON

## ACTION:

I listen to my inner voice when I am confronted with people's actions and statements. Deep inside I know the answers, so I pay attention to my instinct.

## POINT TO PONDER:

For the longest time, instinct was disregarded as something that only animals had. Fortunately, we have become wiser and now accept the fact that we, too, have instincts, and if we decide to follow them, they can lead us in very fruitful directions and prevent us from making unnecessary mistakes. Perhaps our greatest human quality is that of examining our instincts and analyzing where they come from and how they unfold. Under no circumstances should we ignore this precious gift we received from birth.

# June 18

## GUIDING QUOTE:

*Pleasure in the job puts perfection in the work.*

~ ARISTOTLE

## ACTION:

Do I enjoy my work? Am I proud of what I do? I contemplate on these things, gauge my dedication, and figure out ways to improve.

## POINT TO PONDER:

Over the gate in the Obaku temple in Kyoto are carved the words, "The First Principle." Many admire the inscription as a masterpiece. It was crafted by Kosen two hundred years ago. As Kosen initially sketched the letters, a bold pupil who never failed to criticize his master's work looked on. "That's not good," he said after the first effort. "How is that one?" "Worse than before," said the pupil. Kosen wrote sheet after sheet, until eighty-four trials had been accumulated, all without approval of the pupil. Then, when the young man stepped out for a moment, Kosen thought, "Now is my chance to escape his keen eye," and he wrote hurriedly, with a mind free from distraction. "The First Principle." "A masterpiece," pronounced the pupil.

*(Adopted from "101 Zen Stories")*

# June 19

### GUIDING QUOTE:
*Always do right. This will gratify some people and astonish the rest.*
~ MARK TWAIN

### ACTION:
I aim to do right—today and every other day. I perform correctly at work and go an extra mile. I help colleagues, loved ones, and strangers in need. I am proactive, and refrain from destructive activities.

### POINT TO PONDER:
When we work in an unethical or unpleasant environment, it is harder to continue doing the right thing, simply because the local culture does not endorse it. Yet, we should continue examining our actions and question our performance at the end of each day: what did we do right, and where did we go wrong? How can we better ourselves tomorrow? It may astonish many people if we insist on doing the right thing, but it is also an investment in a peaceful and contented future.

# June 20

## GUIDING QUOTE:

*Always forgive your enemies; nothing annoys them so much.*

~ OSCAR WILDE

## ACTION:

Today, I let go any sense of anger, frustration, and disappointment in others. By setting these people and memories free, I free myself. Freeing myself means paving the way to new beginnings and more rewarding future relationships.

## POINT TO PONDER:

Everything is our own perception. When we stop seeing enemies as enemies, they are no longer a threat to our health or well-being. They become insignificant in the total scene of our lives, and they will soon fade away. Those among our enemies who really had a problem with us will have to deal with our decision to move on and will feel insignificant. This, then, is their own problem, not ours. Our concern should be to remain free from internal turmoil. Forgiveness helps us bring that about.

# June 21

### GUIDING QUOTE:
*Be great in act, as you have been in thought.*
~ WILLIAM SHAKESPEARE

## ACTION:
I focus on my collaboration skills. I am a team player and share my insights with others without worrying about their possible motives. I am generous and focused in my acts, and leave the rest up to existence.

## POINT TO PONDER:
A martial arts student approached his teacher with a question. "I'd like to improve my knowledge of the martial arts. In addition to learning from you, I'd like to study with another teacher in order to learn another style. What do you think of this idea?" "The hunter who chases two rabbits," answered the master, "catches neither one."

*(Adopted from John Suler, "Zen Stories to Tell Your Neighbors")*

# June 22

**GUIDING QUOTE:**

*Manifest plainness,*
*Embrace simplicity,*
*Reduce selfishness,*
*Have few desires.*

~ LAO TZU

**ACTION:**

I remain myself, so I do not feel unnatural and I do not have to remember any specific attitude. I practice more giving and less taking.

**POINT TO PONDER:**

We are programmed to be selfish and have learned to ignore it. We practice selfishness with such grace that we deceive even ourselves. Yet, in our quiet moments, we can see through the layers of our acts and realize our true motives. Those quiet moments should help us reformulate our driving motives. If we act simply, life will be easier. If we give more, we will feel lighter and warmer inside. If we restrain our desires, we do not become enslaved by them and we maintain our health. Life can be good.

# June 23

*The secret of being miserable is to have leisure to bother about whether you are happy or not. The cure for it is occupation.*
~ GEORGE BERNARD SHAW

## ACTION:

My activities prevent me from feeling useless. I am grateful and happy, because I have something constructive to do. I view my work as a constructive act and am joyful.

## POINT TO PONDER:

The greatest complainers are those who have time to dwell on their many reasons to complain. They complain themselves to distraction, when there could be a useful alternative—engaging in something useful. Whether it is art, education, or handwork, having an occupation makes life sensible. Our occupation does not have to be rewarded with large sums of money. The engagement in this occupation is a reward unto itself.

# June 24

**GUIDING QUOTE:**

*They can conquer who believe they can.*

~ VIRGIL

**ACTION:**

My abilities lie in my beliefs. I get where I want to because I belief I can. Today, I set the first step on my way to the goals I want to reach in my career.

**POINT TO PONDER:**

The greatest leaders are those with confidence. It is this confidence that sets them apart from followers who do not think they are able to do anything without guidance. It is all in the mind. The mind shapes the attitude. If we continuously think that we are worthless, we become just that. If we think we are fabulous, we can also become that. If we think we can conquer a position or activity in the future, we can. Our actions need to be geared toward realizing our goal, and suddenly, it is possible.

# June 25

*The mediocre teacher tells. The good teacher explains.*
*The superior teacher demonstrates. The great teacher inspires.*
~ WILLIAM ARTHUR WARD

**ACTION:**

I have a choice. Which one of the teachers would I like to be in my daily life? I want to inspire everyone I encounter and leave a lasting impression. I turn inward for the right, genuine words toward those I encounter today.

**POINT TO PONDER:**

Inspiring others is one of the greatest rewards one can get. You do not have to inspire entire crowds. If you can inspire only one person, you have done your life's work. Transfer the flame of zest and zeal in life; make others also want to live; let them look at you and think, I want what he or she has—love, peace, determination, resilience, and a positive attitude. Inspiration is like a double-edged sword—by inspiring others, we also inspire ourselves.

# June 26

## ACTION:

Have I attained the level of freedom I enjoy? Or am I merely following guidelines, advisements, and faded dreams that do not really matter to me anymore? How consciously have I made my decisions? Today, I review my freedom.

## POINT TO PONDER:

Many people in many societies think that they are free, because they are told that they are. However, a quick review tells us that most people are not. Civilization has rules and regulations that we all adhere to. However, within those confinements, we can still enjoy a sense of freedom if we make conscious choices on the things we do and the way we live. There are still too many people who live the way they were told to live. They do not do what they really like. They are not really content. That is a waste of what could be a great life.

# June 27

## GUIDING QUOTE:
*Never discourage anyone...who continually makes progress,*
*no matter how slow.*

~ PLATO

## ACTION:
I take this statement to heart and encourage everyone, especially the slow movers.
I reflect on myself and practice patience with the progress that does not happen
as quickly as I had hoped.

## POINT TO PONDER:
Not all ventures develop as rapidly as we envision them. Not all people move as
quickly as we would want them. Not all decisions can be made as swiftly as we
want to have them made. This is part of the fascination of life—the fact that we
have to adapt to different levels of progress. We learn patience, resilience, and
understanding as we go through these seeming setbacks. Too often we become
disheartened or even angry when others do not reason, move, or learn as quickly
as we do. Instead, we should empower them and accept them as they are.

# June 28

## GUIDING QUOTE:

*Battle not with monsters, lest ye become a monster,*
*and if you gaze into the abyss, the abyss gazes also into you.*
~ FRIEDRICH NIETZSCHE

## ACTION:

I am cautious about the politics at my workplace. I make sure that I do not engage in gossip, backstabbing, or other mean practices that are so easy to fall into. Today the joke is on someone else; tomorrow it may be on me.

## POINT TO PONDER:

Those who engage in office politics often do not realize that they lose more than they gain, because the positions and status they are after are only temporary. Their soul and mind, however, are with them long after the job-related primers are gone. That is when they will realize how their mean-spirited actions had been eating at their long-term psychological well-being. When you engage in snakelike behavior, you attract only other snakes and their predators.

# June 29

*He can compress the most words into the smallest ideas of any man I ever met.*

~ ABRAHAM LINCOLN

## ACTION:

I pay attention to what I say. Am I full of empty words, or do I follow up on my promises? How do my colleagues look at me? Moreover, how do I perceive myself? Today, I do not waste words, but act.

## POINT TO PONDER:

We live in a society where eloquence seems to be all that matters, even if it is filled with hollow promises and meaningless words. We can all think of someone like the one Lincoln described above: broad talkers with narrow content. It is unfortunate that many supervisors and managers do not see through that, but often reward the ones with the big words, impressed by their outspokenness, without examining in depth what these big talkers achieve otherwise.

# June 30

## GUIDING QUOTE:

*Appreciation is a wonderful thing: It makes what
is excellent in others belong to us as well.*

~ VOLTAIRE

## ACTION:

I show my appreciation to those who deserve it; especially those to whom I have never expressed it. By showing them my appreciation, we may connect, and their achievements may also become my sources of pride.

## POINT TO PONDER:

During our busy days we often forget to express our gratitude and appreciation to those who have done something right. We often assume that they will understand, but fail to realize how much it may mean to them to hear a word of approval from us. The easiest way to understand this is to reflect. We like it when others express their gratitude and admiration for things we have accomplished. Why not set a good example and ignite a trend of appreciation? Today is a great day to start!

*July*

# July 1

### GUIDING QUOTE:
*He who has begun has half-done. Dare to be wise; begin!*
~ HORACE

## ACTION:
I realize that the right moment for any new project is now, and not at some other perfect time that never comes. I stop postponing, and start today!

## POINT TO PONDER:
The hardest part of every undertaking is to get going. That is why many great ideas remain just that—ideas. We often look up to people whom we consider successful. The only difference between them and us is that they dared to begin, and they did not give up when times got tough. This is another challenge that many do not overcome: going through the hard times that inevitably accompany the fulfillment of our dreams. The key is to be creative and hold on, but it all starts with starting.

# July 2

## GUIDING QUOTE:

*I object to violence because when it appears to do good,*
*the good is only temporary; the evil it does is permanent.*

~ MAHATMA GANDHI

## ACTION:

I focus on peace, not violence. I am honest but gentle to those I encounter, hoping they will be the same to me.

## POINT TO PONDER:

There once lived a great warrior. Though quite old, he still was able to defeat any challenger. One day an infamous young warrior arrived. He was determined to defeat the great master. Along with his strength, he had an uncanny ability to spot and exploit any weakness in an opponent. He was undefeated. The old master accepted the young warrior's challenge. As they squared off, the young warrior began to hurl insults at the old master. He spit in his face. For hours he went on cursing. But the old warrior remained calm. Finally, the young warrior left, feeling shamed. The students asked the old master, "How did you drive him away?" "If someone comes to give you a gift and you do not receive it," the master replied, "to whom does the gift belong?"

# July 3

## GUIDING QUOTE:

*If we cannot end now our differences, at least we can help make the world safe for diversity.*

~ JOHN F. KENNEDY

## ACTION:

Wherever my colleagues, customers, or other counterparts come from, I respect them for their uniqueness, and do not allow myself to fall into the trap of ethnocentric thinking. I embrace diversity.

## POINT TO PONDER:

Diversity has been present since humanity came into existence, yet it has always been an issue of contention. We seek distinctions in race, ethnicity, age, ability, education, sexual preference, gender, and whatever else we can find to convince ourselves of our superiority over others. Even if we do not proclaim superiority, we have a tendency to think that our ways are better than others'. Getting ourselves over that silly idea, and embracing others, is the first step toward greatness.

# July 4

## GUIDING QUOTE:

*All the darkness in the world cannot extinguish the light of a single candle.*

~ SAINT FRANCIS OF ASSISI

## ACTION:

My positive actions may seem to go unnoticed, but they still bring light in the whole of existence. I am a candle; I respect and honor the influences of my performance, realizing that my actions will not be lost in the void.

## POINT TO PONDER:

It is hard to perform righteously and compassionately in an environment where others do not engage in such behavior. You become an outcast and may even be chased away. Yet, you do not have to play along in any game that does not meet your values. You can still do the right thing, even if no one seems to be grateful. Ultimately, there will be a turnaround in your life, perhaps not from this particular workplace, but definitely somewhere. Do not give up—continue to shine your candle's light.

# July 5

### GUIDING QUOTE:

*Learn to adjust yourself to the conditions you have to endure, but make a point of trying to alter or correct conditions so that they are most favorable to you.*

~ WILLIAM FREDERICK BOOK

### ACTION:

I am flexible and creative, and lay out my plan for a prosperous new year—no matter what the calendar says.

### POINT TO PONDER:

A chihuahua got lost and found himself in an African jungle. He soon encountered a hungry leopard. Realizing his dilemma, the dog quickly settled down to chew on some fresh bones on the ground, and, when the leopard was about to leap, sighed loudly, "Boy, that was one delicious leopard. I wonder if there are any more around here?" The leopard stopped mid-stride and slinked away into the trees. A monkey saw everything and ran behind the leopard to tell him the truth, but the chihuahua had seen him take off and was prepared. As soon as he saw the angry leopard approaching again, he exclaimed, "Now where's that monkey gone? I sent him ages ago to bring me another leopard…."

# July 6

*If one speaks or acts with a cruel mind, misery follows,
as the cart follows the horse; if one speaks or acts with a pure mind,
happiness follows, as a shadow follows its source.*

~ The Dhammapada

## Action:

I am watchful of my words and speak with a clear, pure mind. This makes me feel content at the end of the day, and leads to even better feelings in the future.

## Point to Ponder:

When bad things happen to people, we never know their purpose. These bad things may happen to help the person grow, or they may be a consequence of their prior behavior. It is not for us to determine, but the person involved will know. We often speak untruthfully without considering the consequences of such words. Hypocrisy or harsh language falls into the same category of speaking with a cruel mind; they reliably lead to misery.

# July 7

**GUIDING QUOTE:**

*Minds, like bodies, will often fall into a pimpled,
ill-conditioned state from mere excess of comfort.*

~ CHARLES DICKENS

**ACTION:**

I often worry about the condition of my body, but how often do I pay attention to the condition of my mind? Today I do that. I contemplate on the state of my mind and become more alert to ways to use it.

**POINT TO PONDER:**

We have a tendency to ignore our mind and let it do what it has always done automatically, without control. Few of us think regularly about our mind, or consider its condition as carefully as we do our body's. Our mind is precious, and we should treat it as such. Like our body, our mind requires a balance of exercise and rest. Meditation, or just some quiet time in nature, can work wonders in rejuvenating our thought processes. Simple actions can lead to a healthier, more supple mind.

# July 8

## GUIDING QUOTE:

*Let no one ever come to you without leaving better and happier.*

~ MOTHER TERESA

## ACTION:

I make sure that those who talk to me leave with a sense of accomplishment and a heart at ease. To attain that, I listen, not just with my eyes and mind, but also with my heart and emotions.

## POINT TO PONDER:

If we could all ingrain this thought in our minds and live it day by day, the world would be a much better place, starting with our interactions at home and at work, and spreading to larger environments such as cities, states, and nations. But even if it has not happened so far, why can't we, who read this, decide to adopt this wonderful mind-set from now on? Why would it be too late? Think of the great feelings that such conduct elicits—not only for others, but for you as well. Let us do it!

# July 9

### GUIDING QUOTE:

*It is with our passions, as it is with fire and water;*
*they are good servants but bad masters.*

~ AESOP

### ACTION:

I examine my passions and question myself about the degree to which I maintain them. Am I in control, or are they? If I find out that I have allowed my passions to control me, then this is the day that it ends.

### POINT TO PONDER:

It is, indeed, nice to have a hobby, or to pursue activities that stimulate our zest for life. However, we should be cautious of activities that are addictive, for they can become our masters instead of our servants. They may even disrupt our family or our career. There are numerous examples all around us of people who let their passions run away with them. We should prevent ourselves from falling into that trap.

# July 10

## GUIDING QUOTE:

*Perseverance and tact are the two great qualities most valuable for all men who would mount, but especially for those who have to step out of the crowd.*

~ BENJAMIN DISRAELI

## ACTION:

My life is on the right track. I am fortunate to be here, and I persevere to advance even further.

## POINT TO PONDER:

An elderly carpenter was ready to retire. He told his general contractor of his plans to live a calmer life with his wife. The contractor was sorry to see his good worker go and asked if he could build just one more house as a personal favor. The carpenter said yes, but his heart was not in this final job. He resorted to shoddy workmanship and used inferior materials. It was an unfortunate way to end a dedicated career. When the carpenter finished his work, the employer handed him the front door key. "This is your house," he said, "my gift to you." The carpenter was shocked! What a shame! If only he had known he was building his own house, he would have done it so differently.

# July 11

*Die when I may, I want it said by those who knew me best that I always plucked a thistle and planted a flower where I thought a flower would grow.*

~ ABRAHAM LINCOLN

## ACTION:

I seize any opportunity I see, as it may be the beginning of a great new trend or venture. Yet, I make sure that the new projects I engage in are flowers and not thorns to humanity.

## POINT TO PONDER:

Making the best of any situation is an art that takes time to master. It requires courage to move obstacles out of the way, and even more bravery to engage in new acts, especially because there are so many challenges around. Yet, trying is the key, and we owe it to ourselves and generations to come, to plant the flowers that will bloom into great new missions in the future. We should never forget that we are living in the good old days of the future, and that coming generations will look up to us, just like we do to generations before.

# July 12

## GUIDING QUOTE:

*Imagination is more important than knowledge. For knowledge is limited to all we now know and understand, while imagination embraces the entire world, and all there ever will be to know and understand.*

~ ALBERT EINSTEIN

## ACTION:

I look at the things I usually see in a new light. I do something that I do not usually do, read a book I do not usually read, talk to someone I do not usually talk to. I pique my imagination to reach greater heights.

## POINT TO PONDER:

Everything we take for granted today and enjoy without further thinking was once mere imagination. It took confidence, perseverance, and persuasion to materialize all these things into what they are today. Yet, they serve humanity in ways we cannot start to express. Daring to dream, and dream big, is what it all starts with. Who says that dreaming is ridiculous? Ignore those people, and please continue to dream up the next big thing for humankind.

# July 13

## GUIDING QUOTE:

*To put the world right in order, we must first put the nation in order; to put the nation in order, we must first put the family in order; to put the family in order, we must first cultivate our personal life; we must first set our hearts right.*

~ CONFUCIUS

## ACTION:

I set my heart right and review what could improve in my personal life. Then I work on it, in belief that it will also positively affect my other areas of my performance.

## POINT TO PONDER:

A boy was walking along a beach at low tide, where countless starfish, having been washed up on the beach, were stranded and doomed to perish. A man watched as the boy picked up individual starfish and took them back into the water. "I can see you're being very kind," said the man, "but there must be thousands of them; it can't possibly make any difference." Unaffected by the man's negativity, the boy picked up another starfish, threw it in the sea and said, "It just did for that one."

# July 14

## GUIDING QUOTE:

*A man will renounce any pleasures you like*
*but he will not give up his suffering.*
~ GEORGE IVANOVITCH GURDJIEFF

## ACTION:

I consider the things I do not enjoy yet continue doing: tasks, relationships, and habits. No longer do I ignorantly submit to my suffering. Today, I liberate myself.

## POINT TO PONDER:

One can wonder why we have more trouble giving up on our suffering than our pleasures. Is this because we think that our suffering is part of who we are? Is this because our culture demands it? Or is it just our lack of confidence that inhibits us from making the step toward liberation from our suffering? What is it that we fear? Worse situations than the ones we're in? Are we threatened by those who benefit from our situation? Even that can be ended, if we choose for our well-being.

# July 15

**GUIDING QUOTE:**

*Freedom from the desire for an answer is essential
to the understanding of a problem.*

~ JIDDU KRISHNAMURTI

**ACTION:**

I open myself for acceptance. I cease to continuously try changing the world and the people around me. Instead, I try to understand them. This is how I approach problems as well.

**POINT TO PONDER:**

When we open ourselves to understand, we have not merely acquired the capacity to solve one problem, but we have gained precious insight into the nature of the issue, and have enriched ourselves with understanding that may transform enemies to friends, and problems to opportunities. Understanding helps us to shift our paradigm: we suddenly see the reasons behind certain behaviors and circumstances, and we learn to be compassionate. Compassion, then, brings us so much further than an impractical sense of solving an issue at any cost.

# July 16

## GUIDING QUOTE:

*The most precious gift we can offer others is our presence.*
*When mindfulness embraces those we love, they will bloom like flowers.*

~ THICH NHAT HANH

## ACTION:

I am mindful toward my partner, and all those who surround me. I show them my affection through my undivided attention. My loved ones deserve my attention.

## POINT TO PONDER:

The demands of our daily life often place us in time constraints. We travel, work, and engage in social requirements that diminish the time and attention we should give to our loved ones. Oftentimes we think that they will understand, and oftentimes we do not realize how much they suffer from our lack of attention. We miss precious moments from their lives, which we will later regret. It is good to stop and think on that now and then, and express our love in word and deed to those who matter to us most.

# July 17

**GUIDING QUOTE:**

*If your actions inspire others to dream more, learn more,*
*do more and become more, you are a leader.*

~ JOHN QUINCY ADAMS

**ACTION:**

I am a source of inspiration to anyone I meet or communicate with. I am the leader of my life, and I am content when I can serve.

**POINT TO PONDER:**

Two sons worked for their father on the farm. The younger brother had been given more responsibility, so the older brother asked his father to explain why. The father said, "First, go to the neighbor's farm and see if they have any geese for sale." Each time the son returned, the father sent him off with another question. After 4 trips back and forth, a deal was sealed. Then the father sent for the youngest son, and asked him to do the same at the other neighbor. The son took ownership and brought all answers plus a sealed deal back after the first trip. The father turned to the older son, who nodded his head in appreciation. He now realized why his brother was given more responsibility.

# July 18

*He who fears being conquered is sure of defeat.*
~ NAPOLEON BONAPARTE

**ACTION:**

I overcome my fears, and focus on action. Change happens all the time, and standing still equals falling behind. So I start today with a new project, a new study, a new direction.

**POINT TO PONDER:**

Idleness is not only the devil's playground—it is the surest way to failure and a meaningless life. The purpose of our existence is finding a purpose and making it work. We may fail a few times, but if we persevere, we will ultimately succeed. Yes, there may be others who also head in the same direction, and they may seem faster, brighter, or more accepted. But who says that we cannot make it? The only way we cannot is if we stand still, and that is not an option anymore.

# July 19

*Continuous effort—not strength or intelligence—*
*is the key to unlocking our potential.*
~ SIR WINSTON CHURCHILL

## ACTION:

My continued efforts lead me to the goals I want to attain. No setback discourages me. I continue to move and find creative alternatives where the road seems to be blocked. I persevere.

## POINT TO PONDER:

We often look up to people who are smarter or stronger than us and think that they have been given better opportunities to succeed. We may even get discouraged when we find out that our counterparts along the way score higher in intelligence. Yet, giving up on those counts is like giving away our shot at victory. The key to success, as many great ones have mentioned before, lies not in strength or intelligence, but in perseverance. Just go on when others give up, and you will be victorious.

# July 20

**GUIDING QUOTE:**

*A gift is pure when it is given from the heart to the right person at the right time and at the right place, and when we expect nothing in return.*

~ BHAGAVAD GITA

**ACTION:**

I do today what I should do more often: show my appreciation to my colleagues and neighbors, to all whom I encounter daily. A compliment or a little gift does not make me poor, but rich, so I give from the heart.

**POINT TO PONDER:**

People often see giving as diminishing what they have. Is that really true? When we give, especially when it comes from our heart, we feel warm inside. What kind of loss is that? How about giving something small to those we care about today—not for the value of the gift, but for the message behind it? Let us show that we realize the value of these people in our lives. Let us give from the heart.

# *July 21*

## GUIDING QUOTE:
*Insight, I believe, refers to the depth of understanding that comes by setting experiences, yours and mine, familiar and exotic, new and old, side by side, learning by letting them speak to one another.*
~ MARY CATHERINE BATESON

## ACTION:

I lay my perspectives alongside those of my colleagues at work and learn from the interaction.

## POINT TO PONDER:

A group was touring a mental hospital. One of the visitors made insulting remarks about the patients. After the tour, the visitors were introduced to the staff. The rude visitor asked Bill, a security guard, "Are they all raving loonies in here then?" "Only the ones who fail the test," said Bill. "What's the test?" said the man. "Well, we show them a bathtub full of water, a bucket, a jug, and an egg-cup, and ask them what's the quickest way to empty the bath," said Bill. "Oh I see—the normal ones know it's the bucket, right?" "No," said Bill, "The normal ones say to pull out the plug. Should I check when there's a bed free for you?"

*(Adopted from www.businessballs.com)*

# July 22

*You can avoid reality, but you cannot avoid the consequences of avoiding reality.*

~ AYN RAND

## ACTION:

If I try to escape from my worries, they will only augment. I face my problems and work toward understanding them. I know I will be happy once I have resolved them.

## POINT TO PONDER:

Unwillingness to face our daily issues does not make them go away. On the contrary, when we try to escape our troubles, they usually become greater and harder to resolve. It takes greatness and determination to face problems right away, but doing so keeps them from growing. The moment we start working on the organization of our reality, the better our chance to make it gratifying.

# July 23

## GUIDING QUOTE:

*An unemployed existence is a negotiation worse than death itself because to live means to have something definite to do...a mission to fulfill...and in the measure in which we avoid setting our life to something, we make it empty.... Human life, by its very nature, has to be dedicated to something.*

~ JOSE ORTEGA Y GASSET

## ACTION:

I devote my time to constructive matters. I question myself as to whether my work is my life's mission, or just a temporary activity. In case of the latter, I will set out to find my life's mission.

## POINT TO PONDER:

Many people wonder what the purpose of life is, and many people have different formulations for this purpose. However, if not the main one, having a mission makes life meaningful. We should always strive to have a mission, preferably one that is constructive for ourselves and our environment. Every human being leaves a legacy; we should contemplate on the one we want to leave.

# July 24

**GUIDING QUOTE:**

*To everything there is a season, and a time to every purpose under heaven.*

~ ECCLESIASTES 3:1

**ACTION:**

I make an effort to understand that everything has its proper time, and that everything happens for a reason. I am content.

**POINT TO PONDER:**

The difficulty in life is losing things without realizing why. If we have been good, we cannot understand why great opportunities pass us by. We cannot comprehend why a promotion, or a wonderful job, went to one who did not even seem to need it as much as we. However, this is only because we lack the ability to see the whole picture at the moment. Later on, the "aha!" experience will occur, when we see what it was good for.

# July 25

### GUIDING QUOTE:

*No work of love will flourish out of guilt, fear, or hollowness of heart, just as no valid plans for the future can be made by those who have no capacity for living now.*

~ ALAN WATTS

### ACTION:

What are my motives? Why am I doing this particular job, and living this particular life? Do I enjoy it? Can I do something to make it better, here and now? Today, I think on that.

### POINT TO PONDER:

Many of us are so focused on the future that we forget to enjoy the present. We struggle and strive, and keep our eyes on an eternal tomorrow, without thinking of the fact that life happens here and now, and that tomorrow is not a sure fact. While we should plan for tomorrow, we should also appreciate today, and with that, those who are in it.

# July 26

**GUIDING QUOTE:**

*[One] who is naturally and constitutionally adapted to and trained in some or another kind of making, even though he earns his living by this making, is really doing what he likes most, and if he is forced by circumstances to do some other kind of work, even though more highly paid, is actually unhappy.*

~ ANANDA K. COOMARASWAMY

**ACTION:**

My work should be enjoyable. I should feel that I am adding meaning and quality to my life and the lives of others. Do I feel that? If so, I am fortunate. If not, I look for meaning, even if it pays less. Wealth is not always expressed in dollar signs.

**POINT TO PONDER:**

How wonderful is life when our work fulfills us. While we cannot always be so fortunate, we should always strive for that point. When we do what we enjoy, work becomes our mission and source of pride in life. Why should we settle for less?

# July 27

*People demand freedom of speech to make up for the freedom of thought that they avoid.*

~ SOREN AABYE KIERKEGAARD

## ACTION:

My thoughts are free. I think on the fact that many of my opinions and perceptions are instigated by others and not myself. From here on, I critically review them and think for myself.

## POINT TO PONDER:

What is the use of freedom of speech if we fail to apply freedom of thought? It is not something we think about every day, but many of us just follow trends and processes that we have inherited from others. We discriminate without really knowing why. We hold grudges without having a personal reason. We feel superior or inferior to others, to certain jobs, and to certain places, not because we have a reason to, but because it was taught to us. We should stop that, because it is foolish and backward.

# July 28

*The significant problems we face cannot be solved at the same level of thinking we were at when we created them.*

~ ALBERT EINSTEIN

## ACTION:

I look at my problems from a different angle today. The solution is near, and I only have to remain calm and balanced. Creative thinking comes to me.

## POINT TO PONDER:

A principal was alerted by the janitor that girls were leaving lipstick kisses on the lavatory bathroom mirrors. The more kisses he removed, the more there were the next day. The principal realized this problem needed a creative approach. She invited some of the girl leaders to the lavatories, and thanked them for coming. She referred to the lipstick kisses on the mirrors, upon which some girls grinned to each other. She then stated that modern lipstick required a special cleaning process, so she wanted to show them how they had decided to clean the mirrors from the kisses. The janitor then took a sponge, dipped it in a toilet bowl, and wiped the kisses clean. There were no kisses on the mirror since.

# July 29

### GUIDING QUOTE:

*The artist is nothing without the gift, but the gift is nothing without work.*
~ EMILE ZOLA

### ACTION:

My best performance does not depend so much on my talent as it does on the effort I am willing to invest in it. I give my all today and work hard toward achieving my goals. I perform in a way that I am proud of.

### POINT TO PONDER:

Whatever direction we decide to go in, and whatever talent we decide to explore, we need to realize that it will require a lot of work to achieve any significance. Years of hard work lie at the foundation of every seemingly overnight success. Years of disappointment and rejection too. Yet, the strong ones persevere and do not give up when others tell them their talents are insufficient. They just work harder to prove the naysayers wrong.

# July 30

**GUIDING QUOTE:**

*I find that the harder I work, the more luck I seem to have.*

~ THOMAS JEFFERSON

**ACTION:**

I am aware of the fact that opportunity only knocks on doors behind which performance is the rule. I am a performer, and focus on actions rather than empty words, so that my opportunities may appear soon.

**POINT TO PONDER:**

Whether it is a karmic principle or just a logical sequence, there is indeed more luck on the horizon for those who work hard than for those who just sit and wait. Idleness breeds laziness; laziness breeds uselessness, and uselessness breeds dejection. Even if we have a physical or mental challenge, we can engage in activities that will provide us with a sense of purpose. And the more we perform, the better our skills become, the higher our chance to be recognized, and the greater the reward.

# July 31

**GUIDING QUOTE:**

*Whether you think that you can, or that you can't, you are usually right.*

~ HENRY FORD

**ACTION:**

Today, I demonstrate that I can. My thoughts are a self-fulfilling prophecy. I demonstrate my abilities to others, but most of all to myself. Not tomorrow. Today!

**POINT TO PONDER:**

Lethargy is a terrible disease that people fall prey to when they start thinking that they are unable to achieve their dreams. Some people say that they can't because it's the easiest way out of undertaking action. Others say they can't because they have been made to believe by others that they can't. Yet, history has delivered us many who were not expected to do the things they ultimately did. We can also become the outstanding difference, demonstrating that we can achieve whatever we want to achieve.

# August

# August 1

### GUIDING QUOTE:
*I don't know what your destiny will be, but one thing*
*I do know: the only ones among you who will be really happy*
*are those who have sought and found how to serve.*
~ ALBERT SCHWEITZER

### ACTION:

I make sure that I serve the people I work with in any setting: my co-workers, my customers, and those that I do not immediately deal with, but encounter still. Even if through a smile, I try to make the day brighter for everyone I meet, realizing that there is blessing in receiving but more in giving.

### POINT TO PONDER:

We are so focused on taking and receiving that we forget what great feelings we experience when we serve others, especially when we know that we have helped improve their lives. Yet, it is important to realize that the warmth that comes from serving and giving far surpasses the magnitude and duration of the warmth that comes from receiving or taking.

# August 2

**GUIDING QUOTE:**

*The paradoxical—and tragic—situation of man is that his conscience is weakest when he needs it most.*

~ ERICH FROMM

**ACTION:**

Temptation is everywhere, and it's easy to fall prey to immoral behavior with the excuse that everyone does it. I am mindful of that and keep my conscience strong.

**POINT TO PONDER:**

A wise woman who was traveling found a precious stone. She met another traveler who was hungry, and opened her bag to share her food. The hungry traveler saw the precious stone and asked the woman to give it to him. She did so without hesitation. The traveler left, rejoicing in his good fortune. He knew the stone was worth enough to give him security for a lifetime. But a few days later he came back to return the stone to the wise woman. "I've been thinking," he said. "I know how valuable the stone is, but I give it back in the hope that you can give me something even more precious. Give me what you have within you that enabled you to give me the stone."

*(Adopted from Bob Gould, Admirers of HH the Dalai Lama Yahoo! group)*

# August 3

*We all live with the objective of being happy;*
*our lives are all different and yet the same.*
~ ANNE FRANK

## ACTION:

The awareness that everyone wants to be happy will be my guiding thought today. I embrace my family, co-workers, and all others I am in touch with, and try to understand them before judging their behavior.

## POINT TO PONDER:

While we all have our own story, and while we may differ in any possible way, we also have one main common factor that connects us: we are human beings, living on the same planet, trying to make this life as rewarding as possible. Yet, misfortune leaves some disappointed and bitter along the way. We should try to understand where they come from in reflection to our own mishaps. We are still connected.

# August 4

## GUIDING QUOTE:

*Don't waste life in doubts and fears; spend yourself on the work before you, well assured that the right performance of this hour's duties will be the best preparation for the hours and ages that will follow it.*

~ RALPH WALDO EMERSON

## ACTION:

My dedication to my work is sharp and high today. Every task I fulfill is an important foundation of my future. This is where my motivation comes from. I cherish that thought.

## POINT TO PONDER:

Too much talking leaves too little time for doing. Endless reasoning whether we're on the right path will never get us there. Our actions are the driving force that ultimately helps us get anywhere. Whether our current task is our final one or not, it is important for our future. Everything is a lesson. So is today.

# August 5

### GUIDING QUOTE:
*The more you know yourself, the more you forgive yourself.*
~ CONFUCIUS

### ACTION:
Today, I forgive others. I am not without flaws. My self-reflections and the lessons I have learned so far have taught me that. I could not be what I am today without forgiving myself for all my mistakes.

### POINT TO PONDER:
Forgiveness is inevitable in our lives; we forgive others, and ourselves, and we should know that this will continue throughout our lives. Without forgiveness, life is a lonely place, and our heart becomes a dwelling place for resentment. If we can forgive ourselves time and again, why not do it with others as well? They are just as human as we are and are also destined to make their mistakes. They learn, as do we. When we forgive them, we not only do them a favor, we set ourselves free.

# August 6

*We've been warned against offering the people of this nation false hope. But in the unlikely story that is America, there has never been anything false about hope.*

~ BARACK OBAMA

## ACTION:

Hope is the best thing I have. I have come this far because of my hopes. I will get even further thanks to them. I nurture, cherish, and share hope toward great outcomes, starting today.

## POINT TO PONDER:

How beautiful is hope, yet how ridiculed by many! Those of us who have grown through hope know that it is the strongest guide to success. We cannot reach our goals with only knowledge and organization. Hope for good outcomes and a positive outlook are fundamental. Hope is an old virtue, often underestimated, but it holds tremendous power. Let us instill in each other the power of hope.

# August 7

*It is every man's obligation to put back into the world at least the equivalent of what he takes out of it.*

~ ALBERT EINSTEIN

## ACTION:

I give as much as I can. My gifts are not only material, but also emotional and spiritual. I am kind to my fellow living beings, and work on leaving a worthwhile legacy.

## POINT TO PONDER:

A little girl was ill with a rare blood disorder and badly needed a blood donor, but there was no match. At last, her six-year-old brother was checked, and his blood type proved a match. The mother and doctor explained to the boy how his blood would help his sister stay alive. The little boy asked if he could think about it. The next day, he agreed to give his sister what she needed. He was placed in a bed next to his sister and the transfusion began. Quickly, the color and life began flooding back into the little girl and every one was overjoyed. The little boy then asked, "How long will it be before I die?" He thought that by giving his blood, he was giving his life. Yet, he agreed....

# August 8

*Arguments are often like melodramas—they have
a predictable beginning, middle, and end.*

~ GAY HENDRICKS

## ACTION:

I am peaceful toward my family and co-workers. Arguments require energy that can be applied more responsibly toward other pursuits. Today is an argument-free day.

## POINT TO PONDER:

Arguments are silly and often very costly. A man and his wife had been arguing all evening, and as bedtime approached neither was speaking to the other. It was not unusual for the pair to continue this war of silence for two or three days, but on this occasion the man needed to be awake at 4:30 a.m. to catch an important flight. Being a heavy sleeper, he normally relied on his wife to wake him. Unwilling to break the silence, he wrote on a piece of paper, "Please wake me at 4:30 a.m.—I have an important flight to catch." He put the note on his wife's pillow and went to sleep. The man awoke the next morning at 8:00 a.m. There was a hand-written note on his bed stand: "It's 4:30 a.m.—get up."

# *August 9*

### GUIDING QUOTE:

*What man actually needs is not a tensionless state but rather*
*the striving and struggling for some goal worthy of him.*
*What he needs is not the discharge of tension at any cost,*
*but the call of a potential meaning waiting to be fulfilled by him.*

~ VICTOR FRANKL

## ACTION:

A healthy drive toward meaning in my life is what I ignite today. Where am I going? What is my goal? What is the purpose of my actions, my studies, my work? Today, I contemplate on the meaning of my life.

## POINT TO PONDER:

It is unfortunate that so few people really contemplate on the meaning of their life. What are they here for? What do they want to make of this journey? Are they merely sleepwalking? Many are! What a waste. A meaningful life is so much more rewarding, so much more fulfilling, and so much more blessed. Life's meaning is what we formulate ourselves. We should strive to find that meaning.

# August 10

## GUIDING QUOTE:
*At times our own light goes out and is rekindled by a spark from another person. Each of us has cause to think with deep gratitude of those who have lighted the flame within us.*
~ ALBERT SCHWEITZER

## ACTION:

I express gratitude to the person who most recently inspired me. I send a thank you note to those who inspired me before. I try to inspire at least one other person in return.

## POINT TO PONDER:

A farmer got so old that he couldn't work anymore. He would sit on the porch all day. His son, still working the farm, thought, "My dad's of no use any more." One day the son got so frustrated that he built a wood coffin, dragged it over to the porch, and told his father to get in. The father calmly climbed inside. After closing the lid, the son dragged the coffin to a cliff. As he approached the drop, he heard tapping from inside the coffin. He opened it up. The father said, "Throw me over the cliff if you like, but save this good wood coffin. Your children might need to use it."

*(Adopted from John Suler, "Zen Stories to Tell Your Neighbors")*

# August 11

### GUIDING QUOTE:
*Thousands of candles can be lit from a single candle, and the life of the candle will not be shortened. Happiness never decreases by being shared.*
~ BUDDHA

## ACTION:
Happiness is a great thing: it actually increases when you share it. I share my happiness and positive thoughts with those who surround me today. I try to make them happy in every way I can.

## POINT TO PONDER:
A student of a philosophical school of Buddhism came to the master Gasan as a pupil. When he was departing a few years later, Gasan warned him, "Studying the truth speculatively is useful as a way of collecting preaching material. But remember that unless you meditate constantly, your light of truth may go out."

*(Adopted from "101 Zen Stories")*

Some things are worth being reminded of. In our ego-centered society, we have grown accustomed to keeping things to ourselves. We are reluctant to share, because we fear that others may take advantage of us and of our good intentions. Yet, somewhere, a change has to start.

# August 12

*You will always find an answer in the sound of water.*

~ CHUANG TZU

## ACTION:

Not all answers seem to be readily available, even though they are. They just require attention and deep thought. Today, I seek some quiet space and align my thoughts.

## POINT TO PONDER:

We often engage in complicated activities and calculations to find solutions to our problems. Yet, a moment of quietude with a silent mind can work miracles. When we seek to restore our inner balance, decisions become more accessible. The answer lies in the restored connection with ourselves. Listening to water helps us relax. Dwelling in nature, even if for a little while, helps us to refocus. It's unfortunate that these options do not cross our minds so often anymore.

# August 13

## GUIDING QUOTE:

*Courage is what it takes to stand up and speak;*
*courage is also what it takes to sit down and listen.*

~ SIR WINSTON CHURCHILL

## ACTION:

I listen more than I speak. I do not allow my self-perceived importance get the better of me; I listen to what others have to say. This is how I learn.

## POINT TO PONDER:

Sometimes it seems that talking is a problem rather than a solution. Many people talk without having anything to say. They just utter words for the sake of making sound, and do not even realize how aggravating it must be for the attentive listener. We have grown so enamored with our capacity to speak that we often ignore the beauty of speaking only when it makes sense, and listening in order to give others a chance to express themselves. We should think on that.

# August 14

## GUIDING QUOTE:

*Be polite to all, but intimate with few.*

~ THOMAS JEFFERSON

## ACTION:

I show my respect, kindness, and compassion to all I encounter today. Yet, I remain aware that there is no need to share my deepest secrets with everybody. I practice self-control.

## POINT TO PONDER:

We can be spiritual and still maintain some responsible detachment. When we share all our secrets with others, we open ourselves to be harmed. The art of living is to know when to speak and when to be quiet; when to share information, and when to keep it to yourself. If you do not know for sure if something should be said, wait to say it until you know for sure. This will spare you from regret. Once uttered, words cannot be taken back.

# August 15

**GUIDING QUOTE:**

*Seek not good from without: seek it from within yourselves,
or you will never find it.*

~ EPICTETUS

**ACTION:**

I find the good within me and spread it to the world outside. This way, I contribute to goodness.

**POINT TO PONDER:**

An old master was traveling with a disciple who carried his bags. They saw farmers working. Countless insects were killed in the process, eaten by birds. The disciple thought, "I will become a Buddha and save all these creatures." Immediately the master, able to read others' thoughts, said, "Give me the bags. I will follow you." The puzzled disciple obeyed. The disciple grew tired and thought, "There is too much suffering. Perhaps I should only help myself." The master said, "Now you carry the bags and follow me." The disciple did as told. This sequence repeated itself several times. Finally, the disciple asked why. The master said, "When you had enlightened thoughts, I had to follow you. But when you had selfish thoughts, you had to carry my bags!"

# August 16

*For everything you have missed, you have gained something else, and for everything you gain, you lose something else.*

~ RALPH WALDO EMERSON

## ACTION:

I celebrate my wins, as well as my losses, and realize that they both serve a useful purpose in my life.

## POINT TO PONDER:

We often do not think of it that way, but the balance of life is unique and unequivocal. We win some and lose some: we celebrate and mourn, but there is a time for everything, and everything serves a purpose. People, events, and things come and go in our lives. For every one that comes one goes, and vice versa. It is no use staring too long at closed doors, because that takes away from the time we can enjoy the new window that opened.

# August 17

**GUIDING QUOTE:**

*You have your way. I have my way. As for the right way,*
*the correct way, and the only way, it does not exist.*

~ FRIEDRICH NIETZSCHE

**ACTION:**

I keep in mind that the world is a reflection of us. There are multiple views, thus multiple truths.

**POINT TO PONDER:**

It is highly arrogant and backward to think that one's truth or way of acting is the only good way. This ethnocentric mind-set has been at the core of many wars and much human sorrow. Some people think that they have all the answers and look down upon others, not realizing that their ways seem just as ridiculous to the others. How great would the world be if we would learn to accept and learn from each other's wisdom.

# August 18

## GUIDING QUOTE:

*What matters in life is not what happens to you but
what you remember and how you remember it.*

~ GABRIEL GARCIA MARQUEZ

## ACTION:

My mind is a wonderful gift. It determines the way I see the world. I need to nurture it; yet, I also need to control it. I pay attention to my perceptions.

## POINT TO PONDER:

A distraught man approached the Zen master. "Please, Master, I feel lost, desperate. I do not know who I am. Please, show me my true self!" But the teacher just looked away without responding. The man began to plead and beg, but still the master gave no reply. Finally giving up in frustration, the man turned to leave. At that moment the master called out to him by name. "Yes!" the man said as he spun back around. "There it is!" exclaimed the master.

*(Adopted from John Suler, "Zen Stories to Tell Your Neighbors")*

# August 19

**GUIDING QUOTE:**

*He who controls others may be powerful,*
*but he who has mastered himself is mightier still.*

~ LAO TZU

**ACTION:**

I work on self-mastery: how can I become a better person? What are my flaws? What can I do to serve my surroundings better and make a positive difference?

**POINT TO PONDER:**

When we are in an assigned leadership position, whether at work or elsewhere, we may acquire a sense of superiority. What we should realize, though, is that we could emerge as much greater leaders if we demonstrated self-control and responsibility, even if we were not the official leader. People gravitate to natural leaders—those who do the right thing and contain themselves. This is a thought worth contemplating.

# August 20

**GUIDING QUOTE:**

*Anything is possible. You can be told that you have a 90-percent chance or a 50-percent chance or a 1-percent chance, but you have to believe, and you have to fight.*

~ LANCE ARMSTRONG

**ACTION:**

Whether my chances look good, mediocre, or downright grim, I give my all today. I am the best I can be. I believe in myself.

**POINT TO PONDER:**

Life is wonderful! There have been too many instances in which predictions were defied to allow us to be beaten down by any type of judgment. The human mind is a strong tool that can help us turn sorrow into joy, and failure into success. Miracles are all around us, everyday and all the time. Why wouldn't we be part of a miracle as well? We can achieve what we want, as long as we want it badly enough. We can be our own blessing or curse through the way we use our mind. The choice is ours.

# August 21

**GUIDING QUOTE:**

*What is my life if I am no longer useful to others.*
~ JOHANN WOLFGANG VON GOETHE

**ACTION:**

My service to others gives purpose to my day. I serve happily and make sure that what I do benefits others in a lasting manner.

**POINT TO PONDER:**

While there seems to be gratification in being selfish, there is much more meaning in serving others. There are numerous ways to do this. We can engage in creative thinking and try to find a need in our community. Our work should also be meaningful to the well-being of others. It is therefore important to see the big picture of our activities, no matter how tedious and insignificant our daily tasks may seem. The ultimate purpose should be evident, and from there on we can decide whether we agree with this purpose or not.

# August 22

**GUIDING QUOTE:**
*If I had eight hours to chop down a tree,*
*I'd spend six hours sharpening my ax.*
~ ABRAHAM LINCOLN

**ACTION:**

I prepare well for any task, knowing that good preparation and self-control are key to success.

**POINT TO PONDER:**

One day there was an earthquake that shook the entire temple. Many monks were terrified. When the earthquake stopped, the teacher said, "Now you have had the opportunity to see how a Zen man behaves in a crisis situation. You may have noticed that I did not panic. I was quite aware of what was happening and what to do. I led you all to the strongest part of the temple. You see we have all survived. However, despite my self-control and composure, I did feel a little bit tense—which you may have deduced from the fact that I drank a large glass of water, something I never do under ordinary circumstances." One of the monks smiled, but didn't say anything. "What are you laughing at?" asked the teacher. "That wasn't water," the monk replied. "It was soy sauce."

*(Adopted from John Suler, "Zen Stories to Tell Your Neighbors")*

# August 23

### GUIDING QUOTE:
*Tell me and I'll forget; show me and I may remember; involve me and I'll understand.*

~ CHINESE PROVERB

## ACTION:
I involve my entire being in everything I do today, so that I understand the purpose and the ways I can serve even better.

## POINT TO PONDER:
It is important for us to remember that people feel best about anything when they can be involved. Just listening or demonstrating something only awakens some interest, but no real affiliation. It is the actual involvement that creates a bond. If we want to establish a sense of connectedness with our co-workers, we have to involve them as much as possible in our projects. This is how we create allies, nurture a sense of connectedness, and guarantee great results.

# August 24

## GUIDING QUOTE:

*Man suffers most from the suffering he fears, but which never appears; therefore he suffers more than God meant him to suffer.*

~ DUTCH PROVERB

## ACTION:

I refrain from needless worries today, and focus on success. I keep in mind that my accomplishments stand or fall with my own actions.

## POINT TO PONDER:

Too many people fail to work toward the realization of their dreams because they are fearful of everything that can go wrong. At the same time, they envy the ones who are successful, not realizing that those were once where they are now. The only difference is that the successful people in this world refused to give in to their fears and went ahead with their plans, even when times were hard and the tide seemed against them. Suffering is a part of life, but our mind magnifies the real suffering we endure.

# August 25

### GUIDING QUOTE:
*When you shoot an arrow of truth, dip its point in honey.*
~ ARAB PROVERB

### ACTION:
I am tactful in my statements, realizing that it does not matter so much what I say, but how I say it. I speak the truth, but do so with dignity and respect for the recipient.

### POINT TO PONDER:
While we should not sugarcoat our statements to the point that the recipient only sees the sugar, we should still consider human dignity. We can bring any message in a way that avoids robbing the other party of their self-respect. Even laying off people can happen in a graceful way of mutual respect. We may not be able to eradicate all the pain and sorrow in the world, but we can help to minimize the number of insults and arrogant statements that bring about bitterness and hate.

# August 26

### GUIDING QUOTE:
*He who knows little quickly tells it.*
~ ITALIAN PROVERB

## ACTION:

I am watchful for those who approach me with secrets that only stir up anger, suspicion, and spite. Such people are usually out to create unnecessary havoc.

## POINT TO PONDER:

The above proverb should be taken to heart from both angles: you should be careful in allowing others to stir up the atmosphere by uttering statements that they cannot validate, but you should also keep your lips from speaking things that you cannot confirm. Most people want to impress others and will do anything to achieve it. Sharing juicy stories is a sure way to attract people's attention, to make them think that you are important, and to create chaos. But the reward is dubious.

# August 27

### GUIDING QUOTE:
*Never promise a poor person, and never owe a rich one.*
~ BRAZILIAN PROVERB

## ACTION:
I am vigilant with my actions, words, and thoughts today. Each person I encounter is worth being honest to, regardless of his or her background. I try not to offend anyone.

## POINT TO PONDER:
It is important to know how to stay out of trouble. Promising a poor person is as troublesome as owing a rich one: it is not easy to get either off your back. Why engage in such actions in the first place? Everyone around us should be treated with respect, and whatever we cannot hold true to, we should not engage in. This way, we maintain good relationships, trust, and a sense of peace within.

# August 28

*Seeking happiness is a straight way to misery.*

~ English proverb

## Action:

Happiness comes when I do not seek it. Therefore, I do not chase it today, but realize that it is hidden in the small things, and that it accumulates through the good deeds I do.

## Point to Ponder:

Many people seek happiness and are disappointed, even desperate, because it seems to get further away as they search. Happiness is not a target to aim for—it is a virtue we carry with us all the time. It is just that we are sometimes blinded by influences of society that convince us that we are incomplete and are missing crucial things. When we start comparing ourselves to others, misery stays, and happiness flies out the window. Yet, when we stop focusing on all these need-creating sources, we realize that our happiness has been with us all along.

# August 29

### GUIDING QUOTE:

*Do not put your spoon into the pot that does not boil for you.*

~ ROMANIAN PROVERB

## ACTION:

I stay away from people and things that are not mine. There are many temptations out there, and sometimes they seem justified. But I remain true to my principles.

## POINT TO PONDER:

There was a pupil who was caught stealing. The case was reported to the master with the request that the culprit be expelled. The master ignored the case. Later the pupil stole again, and again the master disregarded the case. This angered the other pupils, who drew up a petition asking for the dismissal of the thief, stating that otherwise they would leave in a body. Upon this, the master called everyone. "You are wise brothers," he told them. "You know what is right and what is not. You could go somewhere else to study, but this poor brother does not even know right from wrong. Who will teach him if I do not?" A torrent of tears cleansed the face of the brother who had stolen. All desire to steal had vanished.

*(Adopted from John Suler, "Zen Stories to Tell Your Neighbors")*

# August 30

## GUIDING QUOTE:

*Listen a hundred times; ponder a thousand times; speak once.*

~ TURKISH PROVERB

## ACTION:

I pay great attention today, and only speak when I am sure of what I want to say. I am not intimidated by the assertiveness of others, but speak when I know that what I will say makes sense.

## POINT TO PONDER:

Speaking before our turn has become a trend nowadays, even leading to rewards for the so-called assertive ones whose many words do not really add value to the discussion. Wise people think deeply before they speak, and they listen to others to make sure of their understanding of the subject. Sensitivity and responsibility are taken much too lightly. Thoughtless words can be harmful. Let us think on that before we speak.

# August 31

### GUIDING QUOTE:
*Little by little one walks far.*
~ PERUVIAN PROVERB

## ACTION:

I do not get impatient if it seems that I make little progress. Any progress is still progress, so I keep going. Today is a day for action.

## POINT TO PONDER:

It is easy to get disheartened when we look at the road ahead and think of all the steps we have to take toward our goal. Therefore, it may be helpful to set intermediate goals to celebrate and have a sense of achievement. Yet, meanwhile, we should also keep on walking and not celebrate too much. Only after decisively marching ahead will we finally stand in awe of our accomplishments.

September

# September 1

### GUIDING QUOTE:

*In oneself lies the whole world, and if you know how to look and learn, the door is there and the key is in your hand. Nobody on earth can give you either the key or the door to open, except yourself.*

~ JIDDU KRISHNAMURTI

## ACTION:

I turn inward to find the answers to my questions. Instead of waiting for others and looking everywhere else, I contemplate.

## POINT TO PONDER:

We tend to ignore or underestimate our own wisdom, because we have grown accustomed to getting answers presented on a silver platter. Even though many of those prefabricated, external answers lead to disappointments, we still prefer them to our own insights. Yet, within us are all the answers to all our issues. The problem is that no one else can teach us this but ourselves. We need to work up the will, courage, and confidence to start exploring within, but the reward will be immense.

# September 2

**GUIDING QUOTE:**

*He who learns but does not think, is lost!*
*He who thinks but does not learn is in great danger.*

~ CONFUCIUS

**ACTION:**

I think on everything that happens today as a lesson, and try to learn as much as I can.

**POINT TO PONDER:**

Once there was a well-known philosopher and scholar who devoted himself to the study of Zen for many years. On the day that he finally attained enlightenment, he took all of his books out into the yard and burned them.

*(Adopted from John Suler, "Zen Stories to Tell Your Neighbors")*

Thinking and learning form an unbeatable pair. Without one, the other is useless. What good is a thought if it does not lead to insight? What good is a lesson if we refuse to think on it? Yet, while this may all make sense, we should wonder how often we actually combine thinking with learning, especially outside the immediate educational environment. The answer is, not often enough. Still, the key to progress in life begins with acknowledging the combination of thinking and learning.

# September 3

## GUIDING QUOTE:
*The best way to find out if you can trust somebody is to trust them.*
~ ERNEST HEMINGWAY

## ACTION:

I give those with whom I interact my trust. I do this with care, and listen to my intuition. The future will teach me whether they were worth my trust or not.

## POINT TO PONDER:

Neither trustworthiness nor deceitfulness are written on someone's forehead. We can try to detect behavioral patterns, research reputations, listen to others, or simply go with our gut feeling, but the only way to really find out whom we are dealing with is to give our trust. It may not be wise to start trusting with a major issue, so choose smaller, less harmful topics. As these work out favorably, we can gradually try something larger. Time tells us the rest.

# September 4

**GUIDING QUOTE:**

*True scholarship consists in knowing not what things exist,*
*but what they mean; it is not memory but judgment.*

~ JAMES RUSSELL LOWELL

**ACTION:**

I think of improvement and evaluate my actions. I refrain from following trends mindlessly. This is a day for contemplation, not sleepwalking.

**POINT TO PONDER:**

There is much to know in the world—too much for one person to ever absorb. There is even too much to know about one subject, let alone all subjects. Yet, when we want to stand out, we cannot do so by merely following trends and rules set by others. We need to review, think, critique, and adjust, so that we can improve and further the steps others set before us, and contribute to the wealth of knowledge.

# September 5

**GUIDING QUOTE:**

*People tend to forget their duties but remember their rights.*

~ INDIRA GANDHI

**ACTION:**

I focus on my duties, and fulfill them with great determination and responsibility. I realize that I have rights, but I have duties too, and only by fulfilling them devotedly can I make a difference.

**POINT TO PONDER:**

How many times have we not heard and seen this? People rising up for their rights, but neglecting their work when it comes to performing. It is a tendency that can disrupt productivity in organizations and even harm entire economies. This mentality is easily adopted, but also easily corrected. We need to reflect more, and realize that when we fail to do our duties, we put our rights at risk.

# September 6

### GUIDING QUOTE:

*Twenty years from now you will be more disappointed by the things that you didn't do than by the ones you did do. So throw off the bowlines. Sail away from the safe harbor. Catch the trade winds in your sails. Explore. Dream. Discover.*

~ MARK TWAIN

### ACTION:

Action will be the name of the game today. I dare to start exploring my new goals and release my fear of the unknown. Today is a big day!

### POINT TO PONDER:

If you ask any older person what they regret most, they will tell you what Mark Twain indicated above: not doing what they could when they could have. Life presents us many opportunities, but the window of seizing those opportunities is limited. We think that it is infinite, though, so sometimes we wait too long. Or we are afraid of a thousand things, and then we forego the chance. It is only much later that we realize the error, but then it is too late.

# September 7

**GUIDING QUOTE:**

*The secret of joy in work is contained in one word—excellence.*
*To know how to do something well is to enjoy it.*

~ PEARL S. BUCK

**ACTION:**

Practice makes perfect. I open myself to learning today, so that I may enjoy my activities even more in the near future.

**POINT TO PONDER:**

There once was a monastery that was very strict. Following a vow of silence, no one was allowed to speak. But every ten years, the monks were permitted to speak two words. After spending his first ten years at the monastery, one monk went to the head monk. "What are the two words you would like to speak?" "Bed... hard..." said the monk. "I see," replied the head monk. Ten years later, the monk returned to the head monk's office. "Food...stinks..." said the monk. "I see," replied the head monk. Yet another ten years passed. "I...quit!" said the monk. "Well, I can see why," replied the head monk. "All you ever do is complain."

*(Adopted from John Suler, "Zen Stories to Tell Your Neighbors")*

# September 8

**GUIDING QUOTE:**

*I want to stand as close to the edge as I can without going over.*
*Out on the edge you see all the kinds of things you can't see from the center.*
~ KURT VONNEGUT, JR.

**ACTION:**

The risks I take today are calculated, but risks nonetheless. Playing it safe does not open new paths for me. I enlarge my horizons.

**POINT TO PONDER:**

Nothing can be achieved by merely playing it safe. Risks need to be taken, though not to an irresponsible degree. Taking risks stirs our creativity and guides us to greater heights than we ever thought possible. And even if we fail a few times, we still benefit from the lessons. There is nothing wrong with failing, as long as it leads to learning. The only thing worse than failing to learn from our failures is remaining in the center and always wondering what lies beyond the edge.

# September 9

## GUIDING QUOTE:

*I have found the paradox, that if you love until it hurts,*
*there can be no more hurt, only more love.*

~ MOTHER TERESA

## ACTION:

I focus on love as a caring concern for all those I encounter. I transcend my own boundaries and love more than before.

## POINT TO PONDER:

Love is such an overly used and even abused topic. Yet, it means so much more than we usually intend with it. It is far more beautiful than we consider it to be. It is the difference between a world filled with hate and war, and one with peace and serenity. Love is the universal language that transcends the barriers of language and species. Humans, animals, and plants all understand it. Let us love beyond hurt.

# September 10

## GUIDING QUOTE:

*My humanity is bound up in yours, for we can only be human together.*

~ DESMOND TUTU

## ACTION:

I am fully aware of my connection with all life around me. I specifically focus on my fellow humans and keep in mind that we are connected.

## POINT TO PONDER:

Why are we so smart yet so shortsighted when it comes to mutual acceptance? Why is our species so old, yet so inexperienced in the art of caring for one another? Why do we reach such tremendous heights, yet fall so low? Why do we reject other human beings and fail to care? Why do some of us live in abundance and refuse to help others who starve? Is this human? Do we not realize that there is no humanity without human behavior—that there is no human behavior without mutuality?

# September 11

### GUIDING QUOTE:
*We are masters of the unsaid words, but slaves of those we let slip out.*
~ SIR WINSTON CHURCHILL

## ACTION:

My words are genuine, and I make sure that I do not say things I will later regret. I am watchful, because I cannot take back what I uttered.

## POINT TO PONDER:

Four monks decided to meditate silently without speaking for two weeks. By nightfall on the first day, the candle began to flicker and then went out. The first monk said, "Oh, no! The candle is out." The second monk said, "Aren't we not supposed to talk?" The third monk said, "Why must you two break the silence?" The fourth monk laughed and said, "Ha! I'm the only one who didn't speak."

*(Adopted from John Suler, "Zen Stories to Tell Your Neighbors")*

Words often slip out before we can stop them. Moreover, thoughtlessly spoken words have ruined many relationships and have made many people unhappy for a long time. When we get exited, we sometimes say things we cannot account for later on. Better to think before we speak.

# September 12

### GUIDING QUOTE:
*Freedom is the oxygen of the soul.*
~ MOSHE DAYAN

### ACTION:
How free am I? I live in a society with rules. Besides that, how free am I? I work in a workplace with policies. Besides those, how free am I? I am free in my mind.

### POINT TO PONDER:
It remains an interesting question whether we are at all free, given the fact that each civilized society has layers upon layers of rules and regulations. Yet, we can practice and nurture freedom inside. We have the freedom of our thoughts, and we have the freedom to change careers, jobs, and circumstances. We have the freedom to choose our friends and the colleagues we want to get to know better. Most of all, we have the freedom of our attitude. We can always decide whether we want to see the glass as half-empty or half-full. The difference is that of a miserable life and a rewarding one.

# September 13

## GUIDING QUOTE:

*Things you see from there are not what you see from here.*

~ MENACHEM BEGIN

## ACTION:

I am mindful of the fact that there are many perspectives, and that another opinion or viewpoint is not necessarily wrong. I respect and learn from that.

## POINT TO PONDER:

A Japanese master received a university professor who came for some training. The master served tea to welcome the visitor, who since his arrival had not stopped talking about his achievements, his opinions about theories and experiences, and his ideas about a wide variety of issues. The master poured his visitor's cup full, and then kept on pouring. The professor watched the overflow until he no longer could restrain himself. "It is overfull. No more will go in!" "Like this cup," said the master, "you are full of your own opinions and speculations. How can I teach you anything unless you first empty your cup?"

# September 14

*Look at a day when you are supremely satisfied at the end.*
*It's not a day when you lounge around doing nothing;*
*it's when you've had everything to do, and you've done it.*

~ Margaret Thatcher

## Action:

I do my best to complete my tasks, so that I can look back with a sense of satisfaction and gratitude at the end. I do not complain when I have a lot to do.

## Point to Ponder:

Have you ever wanted to enjoy a vacation, and then found yourself being utterly bored within a few days? Busy people love being active. They feel guilty and empty when there is nothing to do. That is no sin. It is a blessing to have things to do. Being idle too much of the time creates room for wayward thoughts and actions. In being active lies growth as well. You learn as you do. We should all try to remain constructively busy. This is how we can help our world improve.

# September 15

**GUIDING QUOTE:**

*Trust yourself. Create the kind of self that you will be happy to live with all your life. Make the most of yourself by fanning the tiny, inner sparks of possibility into flames of achievement.*

~ GOLDA MEIR

**ACTION:**

My destiny lies in my own hands. My actions and thoughts determine my path through life. I am the self I can be proud of when I am 90.

**POINT TO PONDER:**

We often think that the circumstances around us determine our success in life. But is that so? How many people who went through miserable lives did not turn their fate around and become legends? On the other hand, how many people who were born with a golden spoon in their mouth did not turn out to be pitiful? Indeed, circumstances can help or harm, but the ultimate decision as to how we are going to let our circumstances influence us lies within.

# September 16

## GUIDING QUOTE:
*We can live without religion and meditation,*
*but we cannot survive without human affection.*
~ THE DALAI LAMA

## ACTION:

My focus is on interconnectedness. I perceive my colleagues, clients, and all those I meet as if I see them for the first time, and grant them my affection in every possible yet responsible way.

## POINT TO PONDER:

Living in the world, we are all part of the congregation of living beings. Yet, we separate ourselves through institutions that teach us that we are better than others, and that others cannot possibly be seen as equal to us. We may even keep our children from playing with other children because we doubt that they are the right kind to befriend. Yet, human affection is a beautiful thing that we can learn to bring out toward everyone. Why not try?

# September 17

*The future starts today, not tomorrow.*

~ POPE JOHN PAUL II

## ACTION:

Today is the first day of my future. I do not waste that. Being useless and lazy today means starting off on the wrong foot with my future. I do not postpone the start of my future plans.

## POINT TO PONDER:

It is so easy to procrastinate the things we have to do, and think that tomorrow is good enough. Yet, there are always other things to do. You do not have to look at this fact from a religious angle; it makes sense in every area, whether at home or at work. At work, it is particularly important to get into action as soon as possible. Why wait till others have done all the work, and then get upset when we are surpassed for a reward? The universe has a unique way of rewarding us for our diligence. Today is a great day for working!

# September 18

**GUIDING QUOTE:**

*The greatest part of our happiness depends on our dispositions, not our circumstances.*

~ MARTHA WASHINGTON

**ACTION:**

Regardless of others' views, I see my life as a great journey, full of opportunities, and today brings a great one!

**POINT TO PONDER:**

A traveler on his way from one village to another asked a monk who was working the fields what it was like in the nearby village. "How was it in the village where you came from?" asked the monk. "Dreadful," replied the traveler. "The people were cold, and I never felt at home there. So, what can I expect in this village?" "I am sorry," said the monk, "but I think your experience will be much the same there." The traveler hung his head and walked on. Then another traveler came by and asked the monk the same thing. "How was it where you came from?" asked the monk. "It was a wonderful experience. I would have stayed but am committed to traveling on. I felt like a member of the family in the village." "I think you will find it much the same," replied the monk. The traveler smiled and journeyed on.

# *September 19*

## GUIDING QUOTE:

*Be careful what you water your dreams with. Water them with worry and fear and you will produce weeds that choke the life from your dream. Water them with optimism and solutions and you will cultivate success. Always be on the lookout for ways to turn a problem into an opportunity for success. Always be on the lookout for ways to nurture your dream.*

~ LAO TZU

## ACTION:

Whatever disturbing news I receive, I remain optimistic and look for creative solutions. This helps me to get on my feet again quickly and succeed.

## POINT TO PONDER:

Our mind can direct us along various paths. It is up to us to realize, when we sense fear and worry, that they should not remain with us. Only the strong survive. Every challenge is a blessing in disguise. The art is to find the blessing and capitalize on it.

# September 20

## GUIDING QUOTE:

*No man is an island, entire of itself...any man's death diminishes me, because I am involved in mankind; and therefore never send to know for whom the bell tolls; it tolls for thee.*

~ JOHN DONNE

## ACTION:

My awareness of connection to all people helps me today to serve better, to give more, to help more intensely, and to accept others for who they are.

## POINT TO PONDER:

Awareness is a virtue that can diminish when we are exposed to the wrong vibes. Yet, it can also be sharpened when we encounter the right influences. Wrong vibes and right influences can be found everywhere—it is up to us which of these we select as our source of thinking. Unfortunately, leaders often fall back on a divide-and-conquer mentality in order to consolidate their power. That is why we still have wars, poverty, and other types of suffering. But it is never too late. We can bring a change. Now.

# *September 21*

*Dignity consists not in possessing honors,*
*but in the consciousness that we deserve them.*

~ ARISTOTLE

## ACTION:

I engage in honorable actions. I work hard toward reaching my goals. I assist where I can because I am a great team player. I am genuine, honest, and kind.

## POINT TO PONDER:

Dignity is not something others give to us. It is how we see and carry ourselves. It has everything to do with our self-perception. We do not have to be the boss or possess a lot of wealth to have dignity. Many people who are affluent are not dignified, because they engage in disgraceful acts, speak untrue words, think dark thoughts, or have a sick spirit. Many people who are financially poor hold far more dignity because they engage in an honest livelihood, they do not get confused between appearance and value, and they keep their spirit healthy. Dignity is exuded and can be felt by others who see you. Dignity is timeless.

# September 22

### GUIDING QUOTE:
*A wise man will make more opportunities than he finds.*

~ SIR FRANCIS BACON

## ACTION:

This is a day for creative insights. I look around and try to find opportunities in the things I usually take for granted. How can I improve the quality of my life? I think on that today and work toward it.

## POINT TO PONDER:

Waiting for an opportunity could take forever, because we may not see it when it appears. Some opportunities come under heavy disguise, even in the shape of setbacks. This is where our attitude and the power of our mind come into play. We can seek superficially, refrain from thinking and perceiving at a deeper level, and let a great chance for improvement pass us by; or we can apply some creative thinking and constructive contemplation. Opportunities are ours to make from almost anything we encounter.

# September 23

## Action:

I make sure to learn something new. If I cannot find it in my immediate work environment, I look for it elsewhere. I know there are many things I just see without thinking about. Today, I learn.

## Point to Ponder:

We cannot possibly know everything in the world. We cannot even know everything about one thing. Yet, the enormity of things there are to learn should not dishearten us. We should, rather, focus on what we want to learn, and then devote ourselves to it. If we want to master something, we need to allot at least 10,000 hours to it. If we want to create something new from existing material, we will need to devote a lot of time trying. The greatest inventors endured many failures before they made their big breakthrough. Learning is insatiable.

# September 24

### GUIDING QUOTE:
*Tradition is a guide and not a jailer.*
~ W. SOMERSET MAUGHAM

## ACTION:

I refrain from automatically following traditions and habits without thinking them through. I critically review the traditional behaviors I engage in. I keep the guides and discard the jailers.

## POINT TO PONDER:

One day a young Russian czar was strolling outside his palace, when he saw a guard standing in a barren field. This had been the tradition for many years, and the czar decided to find out why such a meaningless thorny field had to be guarded. He found out that, long ago, Catherine the Great had held acres of beautiful rose-gardens in that yard. The peasants were permitted to view the rose gardens, with a sentry posted to guard the special bushes. Many years had passed since; the rose garden had withered away and become a barren field, leaving a soldier to stand guard over a meaningless tradition.

# September 25

## GUIDING QUOTE:

*Hateful to me as the gates of Hades is that man who hides one thing in his heart and speaks another.*

~ HOMER

## ACTION:

Hypocrisy is all around. I do not contribute to it. Not today, and not any day hereafter. I remain truthful and speak from my heart.

## POINT TO PONDER:

Even the most prominent speakers realize that a speech from the heart attracts many more ears and minds than a predetermined statement of complicated words. This is because listeners can hear the difference between what is meant and what is not, if they care to listen with their heart. In our daily interactions, we should think on that. We can only lead others when they trust the truthfulness of our words.

# September 26

## GUIDING QUOTE:

*The shortest and surest way to live with honor in the world is to be, in reality, what we would appear to be; and if we observe, we shall find that all human virtues increase and strengthen themselves by the practice of them.*

~ SOCRATES

## ACTION:

I walk my best talk. I fulfill the promises I made, and become a better person by doing the things I would expect a good person to do.

## POINT TO PONDER:

Being authentic is the only honorable way to be. It is not always easy, and can even get you in trouble sometimes. Like the boy who went to a restaurant with friends and had his share of the money in his pocket: he had not anticipated that his friends would run without paying, but he decided not to. Even when his staying resulted in some stern questioning from the manager, he remained honorable. He paid his share and what else he could with what he had. The manager gave him all of the money back.

# September 27

### GUIDING QUOTE:
*It's a job that's never started that takes the longest to finish.*
~ J. R. R. TOLKIEN

## ACTION:
Today I start something that I have long dreaded, yet need to do. It may be a task at work, a personal chore, or a social requirement. Whatever it is that I kept pushing ahead in the past weeks, I do not postpone it any longer.

## POINT TO PONDER:
Even the nicest activity or job has some less pleasant parts to it. It is not easy to engage in the things we do not like. Many of us postpone them until the pressure to do them becomes so great that we have no other choice. We procrastinate in order to get our adrenaline rushing in order to get a dreaded chore accomplished. Yet, while we postpone, we are regularly reminded of the pending task and dread it every time we think of it. In sum, the amount of time we waste dreading the chore is often more stressful than timely dispatching the task, so we can move on with our lives in contentment.

# September 28

*It is well to give when asked, but it is better to give unasked, through understanding.*

~ KAHLIL GIBRAN

## ACTION:

I am an emotionally intelligent person. I listen deeply to others and observe what they say and what they do not say, so that I can detect their real need. I alleviate this need in every way I can.

## POINT TO PONDER:

Giving is beautiful in every way. Yet, it shines a heavenly light when it occurs through sensing rather than as a response to a request. We can understand body language better than we think. The only problem is that we oftentimes fail to pay attention. While we lend our ears to one person, we have our eyes and mind somewhere else. That is when we fail to detect the unspoken word. We should pay deep attention. When we do, our reward at the end of each day will be great.

# September 29

**GUIDING QUOTE:**

*Great minds discuss ideas; average minds discuss events;
small minds discuss people.*

~ ELEANOR ROOSEVELT

**ACTION:**

I have a great mind, so I refrain from discussing people, other than if my work requires it, and then only in a constructive way. For the rest, I think and dialogue about ideas on mutual progress.

**POINT TO PONDER:**

One day, a person ran up to the great Greek philosopher Socrates, wanting to share something he had heard about one of Socrates' students. Before this person could share his gossip, Socrates stopped him and asked him if what he was about to say would pass the triple-filter test: 1) Had this person made absolutely sure that what he was about to tell was the truth? The answer was no. 2) Was what he was about to tell something good? The answer was no. 3) Was what he was about to say useful to Socrates? The answer was, again, no. Socrates then refused to hear the gossip. We can all use gossip time to discuss creative ideas instead.

# September 30

*Be silent as to services you have rendered,*
*but speak of favors you have received.*

~ SENECA

**ACTION:**

I do something good for someone, and keep it to myself. I speak of the good things that were done unto me, and am happy that I am able to share it.

**POINT TO PONDER:**

We like to inform everyone about something good we have done to another. Wherever possible, we want to place it on our resume in order to demonstrate how sociable we are. We have grown accustomed to selling ourselves in every possible way. We have come to perceive doing something good to another as a great public relations strategy for ourselves. That is a pity, because it represents selfishness, rather than selflessness. It would be better to revisit our motives and engage in more modest and genuine behavior.

October

# October 1

*The wisest men follow their own direction.*

~ EURIPIDES

## ACTION:

I pay attention to my thoughts. Who, exactly am I following on my way to the future? Who sets the direction and who determines the pace? I am the one to do that.

## POINT TO PONDER:

While it is perfectly fine to follow directions on a day-to-day basis from supervisors or CEOs, it is crucial to realize that each of us should determine our own direction in life. Do not let others tell you where to go and how to do that, even though being open to some good advice at appropriate times can be helpful. It is just that the ultimate direction about what you want to do with your life, how you want to furnish it, and which roads you will take depends on you. You are the one who, after all, has to live this life. No one else will do it for you.

# October 2

*To him who is in fear everything rustles.*

~ SOPHOCLES

## ACTION:

My fears have made me paranoid for the longest time now. I do not allow them to have a hold on me any longer. I do the right thing and do not worry further.

## POINT TO PONDER:

When we have a bad conscience or do not feel at ease in a situation, we fear even the faintest smile that is sent in our direction, worrying that it may be the initiation to disaster. This fear may not always derive from questionable behavior. It may also be a consequence of an unhappy feeling at work, or a sense of not belonging. When you are part of the out-group, you fear that anything can be held against you. Just remember, too, that a place where you do not feel at ease is not one where you want to spend the rest of your life.

# October 3

## Guiding Quote:

*No one ever attains very eminent success by simply doing what is required of him; it is the amount and excellence of what is over and above the required that determines the greatness of ultimate distinction.*

~ Charles Kendall Adams

## Action:

I transcend my boundaries. I do more than expected. I surprise everybody, including myself.

## Point to Ponder:

There was a man who worked at a company and served as office manager. However, he would leave strictly on time every day, never bothering to stay one minute longer, even on busy days. He felt that he did what he was paid for, and that no one should mind his timely departure. He had an assistant who always went the extra mile, and never complained when he was asked to stay a little later. When the assistant was promoted ahead of him, the office manager realized that it was due to his unwillingness to invest over and above what was required.

# October 4

**GUIDING QUOTE:**

*Don't go around saying the world owes you a living.*
*The world owes you nothing. It was here first.*

~ MARK TWAIN

**ACTION:**

I work toward my achievements. I do not expect any favors simply because I exist. I avoid any sense of entitlement and work hard to become an accomplished person.

**POINT TO PONDER:**

There are many people who are convinced that the world owes them everything. They refrain from learning or performing, yet want everything offered to them, simply because they were born. Instead of being motivated by the efforts of others, they want similar advantages without investing a similar degree of skill or time. These people get dissatisfied when they do not get ahead like the hard workers do, but it should be obvious that those who do not strive toward betterment will not attain it. We should remember that.

# October 5

## GUIDING QUOTE:

*Character cannot be developed in ease and quiet.*
*Only through experience of trial and suffering can the soul*
*be strengthened, ambition inspired, and success achieved.*

~ HELEN KELLER

## ACTION:

If I encounter setbacks today, I realize that they serve as lessons. I see any problem as an opportunity, and gain strength from it.

## POINT TO PONDER:

Character can be compared to a sailor: one cannot become a great sailor in calm waters. It takes some storms and tough circumstances to weather in order to develop the skills of a full-fledged, respectable, trustworthy sailor. Character works the same way: we need some setbacks—some mental storms—to develop the qualities that will make our character stand out, and make others want to trust and follow us. For ourselves, the development of character is also crucial, because it will help us think creatively and rise above the median to attain lasting success.

# October 6

*Always bear in mind that your own resolution to succeed is more important than any other one thing.*

~ ABRAHAM LINCOLN

## ACTION:

If I succeed I can help others to succeed. Today, I work on what I consider success.

## POINT TO PONDER:

A young woman complained to her father that her life was miserable. She had one problem after another, and was tired of struggling. The father, a chef, took her to his kitchen, pulled out three pans and filled them with water. In one he placed a potato, in the other an egg, and in the third some coffee beans. After 20 minutes he turned off the heat and asked the daughter what she saw. "A potato, an egg, and some coffee beans," she said. He pealed the soft potato, broke the hard-boiled egg, and made her a cup of rich coffee. He then explained: each of these items got exposed to hot water, yet each responded differently: one became soft, the other hard, and the last blended itself into something wonderful. Which one do you choose to resemble?

# October 7

## GUIDING QUOTE:

*I keep six honest serving-men (They taught me all I knew);*
*Their names are What and Why and When*
*And How and Where and Who.*

~ RUDYARD KIPLING

## ACTION:

If I keep confronting myself with these six guidelines to honesty and improvement, I do not get trapped in unethical behavior. I pay special attention to these six honest servants today.

## POINT TO PONDER:

Sometimes the choice and decisions of the majority may overwhelm us. We then find ourselves going with the flow and failing to ask the questions that could prevent us from deviating from our core values. We should remember, though, that there are environments where unethical thinking has become the status quo. And it may not be obvious to us right away. In order to remain on track with the person we will ultimately have to face when all else is gone—ourself—we should be watchful and ask the above questions internally before engaging in actions we may later regret.

# October 8

## GUIDING QUOTE:

*Religion is doing; a man does not merely think his religion or feel it, he "lives" his religion as much as he is able, otherwise it is not religion but fantasy or philosophy.*

~ GEORGE IVANOVITCH GURDJIEFF

## ACTION:

Whatever I believe in, I bring into practice today. I realize that merely talking about it or attending services is meaningless. I get into action.

## POINT TO PONDER:

How many people do we know who religiously go to their church, temple, mosque, synagogue, or other regular meetings, yet live in contradiction to the rules and guidelines of their congregation as soon as the services are over? You may even know some of these people among your family, friends, or colleagues. The best way to set a good example is to practice what you believe. You do not have to convince others to believe in what you do, but you can demonstrate the goodness of your faith or spirituality by being compassionate, honest, and humble.

# October 9

**GUIDING QUOTE:**

*All ideologies are idiotic, whether religious or political,
for it is conceptual thinking, the conceptual word,
which has so unfortunately divided man.*

~ JIDDU KRISHNAMURTI

**ACTION:**

There is no need for me to keep distance from anyone who adheres to beliefs other than mine. I rise above the pressure from any confining group, and value everybody for what he or she is—a fellow human.

**POINT TO PONDER:**

We learn that our religion is the only way to belief. What many of us do not understand is that it may alienate us from other people who could be a true asset in our lives. In workplaces, some people in power positions try to impose their religion on others. They engage in certain practices that are only common in their church, and thereby place colleagues who do not adhere to their religion in an out-group. This is a sad and shortsighted occurrence, which could never be the intention of any institution dedicated to human greatness.

# October 10

## GUIDING QUOTE:

*Prosperity is not without many fears and disasters;*
*and adversity is not without comforts and hopes.*

~ FRANCIS BACON

## ACTION:

Any disappointment I encounter will serve as a beacon of hope toward improvement. I do not lose hope.

## POINT TO PONDER:

A farmer owned an old mule that tripped and fell into a well. The farmer was unable to bring up the old animal, so he decided that the best thing was to put the mule out of his misery by hauling dirt into the well. At first, the old mule was puzzled, but as the farmer continued shoveling and the dirt hit the mule's back, he had a thought: he ought to shake off the dirt and step up. And he did just that. "Shake it off and step up…shake it off and step up…shake it off and step up." It wasn't long before the old mule stepped up and over the lip of that well. What could have buried him actually blessed him…all because of the manner in which he handled his adversity.

# October 11

### GUIDING QUOTE:
*Among those who dislike oppression are many who like to oppress.*
~ NAPOLEON BONAPARTE

## ACTION:
I am watchful today of my actions. Am I harming any person or group with my actions? Does anyone feel oppressed by my decisions? If so, I change that.

## POINT TO PONDER:
It has always been amazing to see where dictators come from. They mostly originate from oppressed groups. It is unfortunate that, after they bring initial elation, they turn around and make the same mistake as their predecessors. What is it in human beings that makes them love to oppress others? Is it the eternal hunger for power that makes bad leaders turn to oppression once they feel their popularity diminishing? Would it not be wiser for them to consider how to become better leaders and then set everyone free? Are you an oppressor?

# October 12

*The interpretation of our reality through patterns not our own,*
*serves only to make us ever more unknown, ever less free, ever more solitary.*
~ GABRIEL GARCIA MARQUEZ

## ACTION:

I reflect on my life circumstances. Do I see my life through my own eyes or through the eyes of others? What parts of my goals are really mine?

## POINT TO PONDER:

Our ultimate success in life will be determined by our own formulation of what matters to us. What do we perceive as happiness? What do we consider success? What are our goals in life? Many of us define these and other virtues on basis of existing definitions. We simply adopt the thoughts and convictions of others, who may have come from entirely different backgrounds. It is like walking our life's path with shoes that fit badly, becoming increasingly uncomfortable, yet never thinking to try on a different pair.

# October 13

**GUIDING QUOTE:**

*After climbing a great hill, one only finds
that there are many more hills to climb.*

~ NELSON MANDELA

**ACTION:**

I finish the task I am working on and celebrate soberly, realizing that the next task, whether professional or personal, is already pending.

**POINT TO PONDER:**

Life is a sequence of challenges to be resolved. We often think that if our current problem is resolved, our life will become more comfortable. Yet, we keep finding that there is always another challenge in store. It is therefore no use to look too far ahead. It may be much wiser to enjoy the current moment and devote ourselves with determination and positive intentions to the current activity. If we can maintain our mindfulness, we will understand that this is the beauty of life: living in the moment.

# October 14

**GUIDING QUOTE:**

*Consult not your fears but your hopes and your dreams. Think not about your frustrations, but about your unfulfilled potential. Concern yourself not with what you tried and failed in, but with what it is still possible for you to do.*

~ POPE JOHN XXIII

**ACTION:**

This is a beautiful day that brings me many new, unexpected opportunities. I explore these new opportunities and focus on new horizons. Life is good.

**POINT TO PONDER:**

Once there were three trees. The first wanted to become a treasure chest, the second a major ship of kings, and the third a huge tree that everyone would look up to. All three trees were cut, and none of them became what they wanted for many years: the first became a manger, the second a fishing boat, and the third was just laid aside. Yet, ultimately, the first became the crib of a future king, the second the boat in which the king performed miracles, and the third a cross upon which the king was crucified. Their dreams were realized when they least expected it and in entirely unforeseen ways.

# October 15

## GUIDING QUOTE:

*If everyone were clothed with integrity, if every heart were just, frank, kindly, the other virtues would be well-nigh useless, since their chief purpose is to make us bear with patience the injustice of our fellows.*

~ MOLIÈRE

## ACTION:

I do not get angry or upset at those who treat me badly today, as I now know that they are there to make my patience and compassion meaningful. I am grateful for that.

## POINT TO PONDER:

It is a strange realization, to know that even bad habits serve a purpose. Colleagues who gossip or backstab; customers who insult us; bosses who belittle or ignore us—they all are there to polish the mirror of our spiritual intelligence and help us further develop our commendable qualities. We should be thankful for these challenges that help us grow. How could we grow if there were no challenging circumstances and people?

# October 16

## GUIDING QUOTE:

*Just think of the trees: they let the birds perch and fly, with no intention to call them when they come and no longing for their return when they fly away. If people's hearts can be like the trees, they will not be off the Way.*

~ LANGYA

## ACTION:

Desire and aversion are my main problems in life. Today, I practice healthy detachment.

## POINT TO PONDER:

We do not have to be Buddhists to agree that the root of all our misery lies in aversion and desire. We are either miserable from what we want or what we hate. If we can decrease these manipulative emotions, we will no longer be their victims. We will then be freer to make bold decisions, not being held back by senses of greed, prestige, jealousy, or strife. We will be more balanced, and experience greater peace, serenity, and equanimity.

# October 17

**GUIDING QUOTE:**

*When you're deluded, every statement is an ulcer;*
*when you're enlightened, every word is wisdom.*

~ ZHIQU

**ACTION:**

I do not take anything personally. I look for the good in everybody and perceive their statements as wise lessons.

**POINT TO PONDER:**

When performing in the daily work environment, it is sometimes hard not to take things personally. Yet, practice can make perfect. Everything is just a moment. An insult, a compliment, a reprimand, or a pat on the shoulder. They all come and go, and they are all part of life's balance. If we manage to see our days as fluid monents in the wholeness of our lives, we might take matters less personally and have more peace at work.

# October 18

*Luck never gives; it only lends.*

~ SWEDISH PROVERB

## ACTION:

I cherish the lucky moments today, but count more on my work and insights through education and experience on my way to growth.

## POINT TO PONDER:

It seems that some people have all the luck in the world and others none. There may be some truth to this perception, but we all have the capacity to develop ourselves and work with others toward greater achievements. While there is always a small amount of luck needed to get things done swiftly, it really helps if there is proper input and serious guidance. We need to count more on our qualities than on sheer luck.

# October 19

**GUIDING QUOTE:**

*A thieving dog knows itself.*

~ AFRICAN PROVERB

**ACTION:**

I am who I am when no one is looking. I continue to engage in the right thing, even when there is no one else around.

**POINT TO PONDER:**

Even if you never get caught, if you do something unseemly you will still have to live with yourself. Many people underestimate the power of guilt. They first engage in something bad, perhaps in the spur of an angry or lustful moment, and then they start suffering from their thoughtless act. This suffering may ultimately demand such a heavy toll that the deed will seem extremely senseless compared to the emotional disturbance it caused. We should think on that.

# October 20

**GUIDING QUOTE:**

*If the camel gets his nose in a tent, the body will soon follow.*

~ ARAB PROVERB

**ACTION:**

Patience is my main virtue today. Not everything happens quickly. Good things take longer. Yet, I am hopeful, even if I make a little progress.

**POINT TO PONDER:**

Learning patience is a virtue onto itself. Mastering patience is a tremendous asset, yet not easily attained. Once there was a monk who was highly impatient. He could not get along with anyone, as he was always getting upset at the smallest statement that did not please him. He finally decided to build a hut far in a forest to learn patience. After seven years, a lone traveler came across the monk's hut and asked him why he was living so far away from the village. The monk said, "To learn patience," upon which the traveler asked, "How can you do that without anyone around?" Upset, the monk replied, "Go away! I have no time for you!"

# October 21

## GUIDING QUOTE:

*Let your mind wander in simplicity, blend your spirit with the vastness, follow along with things the way they are, and make no room for personal views—then the world will be governed.*

~ CHUANG TZU

## ACTION:

Acceptance is my mantra. I refrain from weighing down my observations with the baggage of my past. I see things in their natural presence.

## POINT TO PONDER:

Most of our problems in this world come from interpretations of what others have said. We see insults where they may not have been intended. We get offended by someone's attitude or appearance. And we take action based on our selfish perspectives. Oftentimes we do not consider the consequences of these actions. Results: arguments, strikes, demonstrations, and even wars. If only we could try to be less judgmental, we might achieve a more peaceful world.

# October 22

### GUIDING QUOTE:

*He who wherever he goes is attached to no person and to no place by ties of flesh; who accepts good and evil alike, neither welcoming the one nor shrinking from the other—take it that such a one has attained Perfection.*

~ BHAGAVAD-GITA

### ACTION:

I am kind and gentle, honest and fair, humble and diligent, and I do not immerse myself in office politics, copy room complaints, or water cooler gossip. I work toward rightness.

### POINT TO PONDER:

It is our capacity to remember that also enables us to become opinionated and judgmental, to generalize and discriminate. We are what we have been raised to be, and we believe what we have been taught to believe. Oftentimes we have no frame of reference other than what our parents, teachers, or peers have told us. When we let go of our prejudices, we are well on our way to growth.

# October 23

## Guiding Quote:

*The world more often rewards the appearance of merit than merit itself.*

~ François de la Rochefoucauld

## Action:

Knowing how unpleasant it is when people judge me on basis of appearance, I do not make this mistake toward others. I accept them for who and what they are.

## Point to Ponder:

There has been—and still is—much suffering and under-appreciation of good people, because too many decisions are still made on the basis of appearances. An ass once found a lion's skin that the hunters had left out in the sun to dry. He put it on and went to his native village. All fled at his approach, both men and animals, and he was a proud ass that day. In his delight he lifted up his voice and brayed, but then every one knew him, and his owner came up and gave him a sound cudgeling for the fright he had caused. Shortly afterwards a fox came up to him and said, "Ah, I knew you by your voice." Moral of the story: Fine clothes may disguise, but silly words will disclose a fool.

*(Adopted from Aesop's Fables)*

# October 24

*Trouble hates nothing as much as a smile.*

~ IRISH PROVERB

## ACTION:

I smile to everyone I meet, and definitely to the person in the mirror. I smile, even when no one looks. I smile my troubles away.

## POINT TO PONDER:

A smile is a good form of self-therapy that also affects others positively. Think of the times you have smiled at other people. Nine times out of ten you get a smile in return, even if you do not know the other party. If you smile often enough, people believe you are fortunate, and even when such may not be the case, you may feel better about yourself. A smile makes you a nicer person, and it lights your own heart up. Keep smiling.

# October 25

*Hope is important because it can make the present moment less difficult to bear. If we believe that tomorrow will be better, we can bear a hardship today.*

~ THICH NHAT HANH

## ACTION:

I am optimistic. I cherish my hopes and believe that tomorrow will be better than today. I determine my future.

## POINT TO PONDER:

A man traveling across a field encountered a tiger. He fled, and the tiger gave chase. Coming to a precipice, the man caught hold of a wild vine and swung himself down over the edge. The tiger sniffed at him from above. Trembling, the man looked down to where, far below, another tiger was waiting to eat him. Only the vine sustained him. Two mice started to gnaw away the vine, little by little. The man saw a luscious strawberry near him. Grasping the vine with one hand, he plucked the strawberry with the other. How sweet it tasted! Living in the moment can diminish the grimness of the future. Hope does the rest. It is a great stimulator of creativity and perseverance.

# October 26

## GUIDING QUOTE:

*All food does not come upon one single dish.*

~ NORWEGIAN PROVERB

## ACTION:

If my expectations are not met today, if I do not make progress as fast as I want to, if I get less recognition than I expected, I think on the fact that there are future days to come.

## POINT TO PONDER:

We often become disheartened by own expectations. We may think of our actions as great individual achievements, while our supervisor may see them as a part of an incomplete whole. It is therefore important to persevere without building our expectations up too high. We should continue performing to our best abilities, and then rewards will follow on unexpected days and in unexpected ways.

# October 27

**GUIDING QUOTE:**

*No one has done good who has not suffered disillusionment.*

~ CHILEAN PROVERB

**ACTION:**

Strengthened by the awareness that all great souls have once been disappointed, I work hard today, and get as much done as possible.

**POINT TO PONDER:**

When we see and hear about great people, today or in history, we always think of their greatest acts. We only learn about their successes, and hardly hear anything about their struggles and strife. Yet, we may rest assured that there were tremendous setbacks in all these successful people's lives. If they could get themselves through the hardship, we can too. Disillusionment serves as an effective instrument toward growth, if we develop the character for it. Why wouldn't we?

# October 28

## GUIDING QUOTE:
*Remember, if you ever need a helping hand, you'll find one at the end of your arm ... As you grow older you will discover that you have two hands. One for helping yourself, the other for helping others.*

~ AUDREY HEPBURN

## ACTION:

I help others and myself at the same time today. Looking for the best way to do so should not be hard.

## POINT TO PONDER:

How beautiful would it be if we considered helping others and ourselves at the same time. There are numerous ways in which we can do that. We could clean up our closets and cabinets, get rid of the redundant clothes, shoes, and other commodities we accumulated over the years, and donate them to a good cause. We can take our co-workers out to lunch, and have a nice time together. There is so much choice!

# October 29

**GUIDING QUOTE:**

*What sets worlds in motion is the interplay of differences,
their attractions and repulsions; life is plurality, death is uniformity.*

~ OCTAVIO PAZ

**ACTION:**

I embrace diversity and differences, realizing how much depth and value they bring in my perspectives. Diversity enhances my awareness. Praise diversity!

**POINT TO PONDER:**

Workplaces are continuously becoming diverse. People travel, and companies do too. They attract members from different societies, generations, capabilities, and education levels. Some people dread working on diversified teams, because they dislike the length of time it takes to get acquainted with people from other backgrounds. Yet, this attitude is shortsighted, because diverse teams perform better, and the learning is deeper for all those involved. It is important to open ourselves up to diversity, because it will only increase from now on.

# October 30

**GUIDING QUOTE:**

*The human heart refuses to believe in a universe without purpose.*

~ IMMANUEL KANT

**ACTION:**

I believe that everything has meaning. I seek meaning in my life and find it in everything I do. I help create meaning at my work by cooperating and showing compassion.

**POINT TO PONDER:**

How dreadful life would be without a sense of purpose. We may not necessarily believe in the same purpose, but most of us agree that life has a purpose. We also know that our work has purpose, which we can detect in the mission and vision statements of our companies. What is your mission and vision? Have you formulated it lately? If not, why not try it here and now? It might provide you with great insight on your current purpose in life.

# October 31

## GUIDING QUOTE:

*Slow down and everything you are chasing will come around and catch you.*

~ JOHN DE PAOLA

## ACTION:

I take a breath and think. How hard have I strived to achieve my goals? What needs to be mine will be mine. I shall remain at ease.

## POINT TO PONDER:

A group of alumni, successful in their careers, visited their old university professor. They soon started complaining about the stresses of work and life. The professor brought in a large pot of coffee and an assortment of cups—some plain, some exquisite—telling them to help themselves. When all the students had their coffee, the professor said, "If you noticed, all the expensive-looking cups were taken, and the plain ones left. Your wish to want only the best for yourselves causes you stress. You all really wanted coffee, not the cup, but you took the best cups…and started eyeing each other's. Life is the coffee, and the jobs, money, and position in society are the cups. Sometimes, by concentrating only on the cup, we fail to enjoy the coffee."

*November*

# November 1

**GUIDING QUOTE:**

*The problem is to find a form of association that will defend and protect with the whole common force the person and goods of each associate, and in which each, while uniting himself with all, may still obey himself alone, and remain as free as before.*

~ JEAN-JACQUES ROUSSEAU

**ACTION:**

How can my co-workers and I work toward a common goal yet still be satisfied and free, each for ourselves? Today, I contemplate on that.

**POINT TO PONDER:**

Workplaces that meet the standards of spiritual performance may be close to the idea presented above. When workers feel happy about what they do, and connected with one another, there is an atmosphere of togetherness and an increased will to succeed as a team. At the same time, each member of the team grows and fulfills his or her wishes as well. Even if we are not part of top management, we can implement some actions toward workplace spirituality: Be helpful. Be kind. Respect your co-workers.

# November 2

**GUIDING QUOTE:**

*Your own soul is nourished when you are kind; it is destroyed when you are cruel.*

~ KING SOLOMON

**ACTION:**

Any task I perform today, any word I utter, any decision I make is an expression of kindness.

**POINT TO PONDER:**

Kindness feels good, not only to those receiving it, but also to the one granting it. A wonderful story of kindness can be found in the Bible, where Ruth, a Gentile, follows her mother-in-law, Naomi, out of loyalty and kindness back to her home city. Both women have lost a loved one: Ruth's husband, who was Naomi's son. Ruth starts gathering leftover grain from the fields of a rich man named Boaz. At first, the people want to send her away, as she is an outsider, but Boaz sees her and is touched by her story and kindness to her old mother-in-law. He marries her and they have a son, who becomes the grandfather of King David. Kindness is rewarded.

# November 3

*All our problems, all our disputes, all our disagreements can be resolved quickly to mutual satisfaction if we address the question.*

~ BENAZIR BHUTTO

## ACTION:

I resolve the problems that arise today by looking into the underlying questions. What caused this? How could it happen? What lies at the foundation of the cause? Then I work from there.

## POINT TO PONDER:

Many people try to find crisis-based solutions to problems. Yet, when the crisis is averted, they fail to question the deeper reasons beneath it, until it surfaces again. Thus, problems are only resolved in a temporary fashion, and the root is never addressed. Major issues may finally develop from structurally mistreating problems and ignoring the real causes. With our human brainpower, we should ask more questions of ourselves and of others involved. We should bring our minds together and ask questions as a group. Structural solutions will then be found.

# *November 4*

*The highest of distinctions is service to others.*
~ KING GEORGE VI

**ACTION:**

My gratitude today comes from serving others as often and as faithfully as I can.

**POINT TO PONDER:**

Serving does not strike us easily as a main purpose in our lives. We want to achieve a lot, distinguish ourselves from others, make a name, skyrocket to fame, and have everyone admire us. We are so focused on ourselves, the idea of serving remains an idealistic but fuzzy dream. After all, what do we gain from serving? What is in it for us? In fact, we have much to gain by rendering service to others: gratification for doing the right thing, gratitude from those we served, unexpected rewards at unexpected moments, and a good feeling at the end of every day. In serving, we stand out because we are part of a small group.

# *November 5*

*In much knowledge there is also much grief.*

~ QUEEN MARIE OF ROMANIA

## ACTION:

What can I do to alleviate the grief that has risen with my increased knowledge? Where can I start? Even if it be small, I make a gesture today.

## POINT TO PONDER:

The less we know, the more ignorant we are. The more we know, the more we realize how ignorant we were, and the more we grieve about the ignorance of the many who will not gain more knowledge to attain higher awareness. Yet, seeing knowledge from an optimistic perspective, we know that once awareness has set in, we can engage in activities to improve the things that are not right. We may not change the world, but we can make a start and persuade others by educating them as well. Grief can be overcome by more knowledge.

# November 6

## Guiding Quote:
*If you believe everything you read, you better not read.*
~ Japanese proverb

## Action:

Some caution in what I see, hear, or read, is in order. I am open to impressions, but I also use my common sense and, where needed, my investigative skills to test the truthfulness behind assertions.

## Point to Ponder:

Obtaining information is great, but you should also be critical in your thinking about its source. There were once three fish in a tank, all seeing the world outside and wondering. The first pressed himself against the glass, but remained afraid to leave the water. The second simply decided to make a big leap, had a great moment of excitement while flying through the air, but then fell to the floor and died. The third fish taught himself to leap high above the tank, and land back safely in the water. He told the first fish: "There is no formula for life. We all need to think for ourselves what works for us, and do that," upon which the first fish started exploring the beautiful plants in the tank.

# November 7

*A gem is not polished without rubbing, nor a man perfected without trials.*

~ CHINESE PROVERB

## ACTION:

Whatever goes wrong in my work does not keep me down: I rise and try again. My previous failures serve as sources to make me more knowledgeable, and as fuel to make me more determined.

## POINT TO PONDER:

Getting disheartened when things do not go our way is part of life. Yet, no matter how disheartened we are, we should always pick ourselves up and try again. If, after numerous attempts, we still do not succeed, we need to reflect on what we want to achieve: is it still useful to us, and will it enhance the quality of our life? It might be that we need to alter our goal somewhat to enhance our chances of succeeding. Creativity is part of the road to greatness.

# November 8

*There are two ways to live: you can live as if nothing is a miracle;
you can live as if everything is a miracle.*

~ ALBERT EINSTEIN

## ACTION:

My day is full of miracles, so I do not need to be skeptical. Life in itself is a miracle, and the fact that I came this far deserves ultimate gratitude. I am grateful.

## POINT TO PONDER:

There have always been pessimists and optimists, skeptics and believers, naggers and praisers. Each of us has the right to choose our group. Each group has its challenging moments. People who always see the glass as half-full will get disappointed sometimes, but quickly rejuvenate themselves, learn their lesson, and move on to another great challenge. People who choose to see the glass as half-empty are satisfied when things go wrong, because that validates their negativity. But they are also lastingly unhappy people.

# November 9

### GUIDING QUOTE:
*The weak can never forgive. Forgiveness is the attribute of the strong.*
~ MAHATMA GANDHI

## ACTION:
I forgive those who have hurt or disappointed me. I grew because of these hurts and disappointments. I prefer to be strong and act upon that.

## POINT TO PONDER:
What we oftentimes do not realize is that when we forgive others, we start healing ourselves. There is a story of a man who had a cruel father who was always drinking, swearing, and humiliating his family. The son wished his father dead—and the father died. The son started feeling tremendous guilt, fearing that his bad wishes had killed his father. Many decades later, a man himself, the son forgave his father, and realized that, in spite of all the bad, the father had also instilled some good traits in him. The picture he had nurtured for so many years transformed, thanks to his forgiveness.

# November 10

## GUIDING QUOTE:

*Two men look out a window. One sees mud, the other sees the stars.*

~ OSCAR WILDE

## ACTION:

My perception may not be the same as others. I am not aggravated by that, but realize and accept the beauty and richness of multiple views.

## POINT TO PONDER:

Sherlock Holmes and Dr. Watson went camping. After a good meal and a bottle of wine, they went to sleep. Some hours later, Holmes awoke and nudged his friend. "Watson, look up at the sky and tell me what you see." Watson replied, "I see millions upon millions of stars." "So what does that tell you?" asked Holmes. "Astronomically, I see millions of galaxies. Astrologically, I observe that Saturn is in Leo. Horologically, I deduce that it is a quarter past three. Theologically, I see that God is all powerful and we are small and insignificant. Meteorologically, I suspect that we will have a beautiful day tomorrow. What does it tell you?" Holmes was silent for a minute and then spoke. "It tells me, Watson, that someone has stolen our tent!"

# November 11

**GUIDING QUOTE:**

*The hardest thing to explain is the glaringly evident which everybody had decided not to see.*

~ AYN RAND

**ACTION:**

There are many things I only see through the forest of my emotional and mental baggage. I try to see things as they are, not how I want to see them.

**POINT TO PONDER:**

A daughter and her parents were once fighting over custody of the granddaughter. The most cruel accusations crossed the courtroom as they were making their statements to explain why they should have custody of the child. Then the judge asked for a picture of the little girl and placed it in the center. He asked the parties to tell him about the little girl. All three people started talking full of love about the little girl, and tears started flowing. Memories from a more peaceful past surfaced, and the parties finally realized that they had to focus on the well-being of what they mutually loved and not on their petty angers toward each other.

# November 12

## GUIDING QUOTE:

*The ordinary man is passive. Within a narrow circle, home life, and perhaps the trade unions or local politics, he feels himself master of his fate. But otherwise he simply lies down and lets things happen to him.*

~ GEORGE ORWELL

## ACTION:

This is the time for me to extend my circle of control. I do not just let things happen to me, but become the writer of my own future.

## POINT TO PONDER:

A Zen pupil was sitting in the lotus position all day, so his teacher asked him what he was doing. The student replied that he was trying to become a Buddha. The teacher then took a stone and started polishing it, upon which the student asked the teacher what he was doing. The teacher said he was polishing the stone until it became a mirror. The student then pointed out that the teacher would never make a mirror out of a stone, upon which the teacher pointed out that the student would never become a Buddha by sitting cross-legged all day.

# November 13

## GUIDING QUOTE:
*When we have begun to take charge of our lives, to own ourselves,
there is no longer any need to ask permission of someone.*
~ GEORGE O'NEIL

## ACTION:
How can I take more charge of my life? Do I need more education? More net-working? More on-the-job training? More self-reflection? I seek the answer today and act upon it.

## POINT TO PONDER:
We may not be able to become fully independent, because there is always a place or person in charge of something that we cannot ignore, at work, at home, or in general society. Being part of civilization requires some sacrifice of personal ownership. Yet, we can reduce the number of institutions that decide how we should live. We can start by questioning ourselves regarding what we do. Do we enjoy it? Is it what we want, or what others have imposed upon us? If the latter, we need to seek relief in changing it.

# November 14

## GUIDING QUOTE:

*The more we sweat in peace the less we bleed in war.*

~ VIJAYA LAKSHMI PANDIT

## ACTION:

No arguments for me today. I keep the peace and try to instill it in those I interact with. I seek to understand and demonstrate compassion.

## POINT TO PONDER:

A Zen master who lived in peace and radiance was widely respected in the village. One day, a beautiful unmarried girl got pregnant, and in her despair told her demanding parents that the Zen master was the father. When asked about it, the master simply said, "Is that so?" The parents were upset at the Zen master, smeared his name, and brought the baby, once born, to him. He nourished the child and raised it well. After years, the young woman finally got troubled by her conscience and told the truth. Her parents again visited the Zen master, this time in deep humility and apology. The master just said, "Is that so?"

# November 15

## GUIDING QUOTE:

*To be yourself in a world that is constantly trying to make you something else is the greatest accomplishment.*

~ RALPH WALDO EMERSON

## ACTION:

I observe myself critically. Are my actions really mine? Are my words really mine? Or am I using the words and actions of others? I think on this.

## POINT TO PONDER:

Authenticity is a true virtue. It becomes even more of a virtue in a society where we are molded into behavioral patterns that may not fit us right, but that are required to progress. It takes internal strength and great self-confidence to turn inward and try to detect who we really are. Some people may not find the answer right away, because they have submerged themselves too long in artificial living. Yet, regular contemplating and internal questioning will ultimately lead to a path of authenticity—a path of freedom.

# *November 16*

## GUIDING QUOTE:

*You have it easily in your power to increase the sum total of this world's happiness now. How? By giving a few words of sincere appreciation to someone who is lonely or discouraged. Perhaps you will forget tomorrow the kind words you say today, but the recipient may cherish them over a lifetime.*

~ DALE CARNEGIE

## ACTION:

My heart is in my words. I express my gratitude and recognition with colleagues, family, and strangers. We are all connected.

## POINT TO PONDER:

Words that come from the heart may be forgotten by the one who expressed them, but they can leave a lasting impression on the recipient. Our encouraging words today may make the difference between persevering and quitting for one, and between living and dying for another. If we have the choice between saying something encouraging or refraining from doing so, why choose the latter? We can make the world a better place with a few appreciative words. Rather than diminishing us, it will enrich us.

# November 17

**GUIDING QUOTE:**
*Personally, I'm always ready to learn,
although I do not always like being taught.*
~ SIR WINSTON CHURCHILL

**ACTION:**
There are numerous ways in which I learn. I do not get upset or impatient when others try to teach me something. I learn.

**POINT TO PONDER:**
Our lessons are not always easy to learn, may come from unexpected teachers, and may sometimes even be unclear. A son from a large family became an apprentice in a monastery. An old monk told him to fill a cauldron with water, place it on a stone, and splash the water out with his hands. The boy thought it strange, but obeyed out of fear of disappointing his family. He splashed until his arms were stiff. Everyday, he had to fill and empty the cauldron three times. When he came home on vacation, his family asked what he learned. He answered that he had not learned anything yet. When they persisted, he got angry and smacked his hand on the kitchen table, which instantly broke in two. That is when he realized the purpose of his tedious task in the monastery.

# November 18

**ACTION:**

Any sense of arrogance that I may feel today, I control with the thought above: I do not know much more than the least learned person, especially when compared to the unknown. There is nothing to be conceited about.

**POINT TO PONDER:**

Perhaps it is a good thing that we do not think too often about all that is unknown. If we did, our humility would strike us down and we might become disheartened. Yet, it is still useful to realize now and then that all our knowledge today does not compare with all that is still unknown and will never be known. One lifetime has turned out to be too short. Multiple lifetimes so far have indicated the same. It may be assumed that throughout humanity's entire existence, there will still be an abundance of unknown. Why are we ever arrogant?

# November 19

*Leadership is the art of getting someone else to do something you want done because he wants to do it.*

~ DWIGHT D. EISENHOWER

**ACTION:**

I am cautious about being selfish. There is enough room for me, but what do I do for others? Today, I perform as a leader and help someone achieve his or her goal.

**POINT TO PONDER:**

There is so much altruism in the above quote. Getting someone to the point that he does what he always wanted is a noble task. Most so-called leaders do exactly the opposite: they let others do what they want, and serve only their selfish ideals with that. Real leaders have long transcended beyond the selfish mind-set. They serve others and their environment to the best of their knowledge, knowing that they will earn gratitude and rewards in due time. They are not concerned enough to ask "what's in it for me," because they know that nature will take care of them.

# *November 20*

### GUIDING QUOTE:
*Nothing in the world is more dangerous than sincere*
*ignorance and conscientious stupidity.*
~ MARTIN LUTHER KING, JR.

## ACTION:
Danger lies in holding on to preconceptions without allowing myself to ponder them. Today, I leave the danger zone and open up my mind.

## POINT TO PONDER:
Ignorance and stupidity are problems in their own right. They can obstruct any pathway toward understanding and mutuality. However, when ignorance is sincere, it is practically impossible to uproot. Similarly, conscientious stupidity is a problem that cannot be circumvented. When people are convinced that what they believe is the only truth, that what they practice is the only way, that what they say is the only word, that what they want is best for all, we face a major problem. The despotic leaders in our world have demonstrated that. The disaster of their actions throws a long shadow over humanity's existence.

# November 21

### GUIDING QUOTE:

*The best thing about the future is that it comes only one day at a time.*

~ ABRAHAM LINCOLN

## ACTION:

I see a new chance to start my future. If things go wrong, tomorrow brings another new chance. Life is good.

## POINT TO PONDER:

Amazing, how a perspective can make or break a person. How uplifting to think that the future comes one day at a time. It indicates that we have many, many chances to shape that future into something wonderful. The number of chances we ignore before starting something serious is up to us. Diligence in performance is a splendid way to guarantee a future that will be worth our while. Our life is in our own hands—one day at a time.

# November 22

**GUIDING QUOTE:**

*You cannot shake hands with a clenched fist.*

~ GOLDA MEIR

**ACTION:**

I open myself to past grief and experience connectedness with my loved ones at home and my associates and customers at work. Life is too short to hold grudges.

**POINT TO PONDER:**

Letting go of grudges frees one's spirit even before it benefits anyone else. Anger, on the other hand, can leave lasting wounds. There was a little boy who lost his temper very quickly. His father gave him a bag of nails and told him to hammer a nail in the fence every time he felt angry. Gradually, the boy learned that it was easier to control his temper than to hammer nails in the fence. He proudly told his father that he had his anger under control. The father then asked him to remove all the nails from the fence. When the boy had done this, the father showed him the holes in the fence and said, "Even when we apologize for our anger, the wounds remain." We should respect others more and clench our fists less.

# November 23

## GUIDING QUOTE:

*Become a possibilitarian. No matter how dark things seem to be or actually are, raise your sights and see possibilities—always see them, for they're always there.*

~ NORMAN VINCENT PEALE

## ACTION:

Life is full of possibilities. I find them in the midst of my setbacks. I celebrate possibilities today.

## POINT TO PONDER:

Of course we face discouragement when things go wrong. Everybody does sometimes. Yet, being down does not mean staying down. After a few days you will have to pick yourself up and get on with life. This is one of humanity's greatest qualities: resilience. We can get up time and again, and work up the mental strength to overcome the harshest downfalls. We can motivate others and ourselves. We can see possibilities, even when all others see impossibilities. Let us be *possibilitarians*.

# November 24

*I think there is only one quality worse than hardness
of heart and that is softness of head.*

~ THEODORE ROOSEVELT

## ACTION:

I nurture a soft heart and a strong head. I am determined yet compassionate on my way. And I embrace my fellow humans.

## POINT TO PONDER:

People who demonstrate a hard heart toward others usually hide a touching story. If only we knew what made them so hard of heart, we might feel deeper compassion for them. Unfortunately, many people are like the tips of icebergs—rarely showing what lies beneath the surface. Conversely, people with a soft head readily demonstrate weakness in crucial areas of their lives, lacking the determination to succeed, and generating an aura of overwhelming hopelessness. Our membership to each group should grant us a capacity of empathy.

# November 25

## GUIDING QUOTE:

*Pennies do not come from heaven—they have to be earned here on earth.*
~ MARGARET THATCHER

## ACTION:

I review my prospects. Where do I go from here? Am I on the right path? How can I earn more in order to give more?

## POINT TO PONDER:

Honestly earning one's pennies is more rewarding than getting them in a deceitful way. One evening a thief visited the room of a meditating master. The master said, "Do not disturb me. The money is in the drawer." Amazed, the thief grabbed the money and headed for the door. "Do not take it all. I need some for food tomorrow." Even more amazed, the thief left some money. "Thank a person when you receive a gift!" said the master. The thief thanked him and left. Shortly thereafter, the thief was caught and imprisoned. After serving his sentence, he became a pupil of the master.

# November 26

## GUIDING QUOTE:

*Education is not the filling of a pail, but the lighting of a fire.*
~ WILLIAM BUTLER YEATS

## ACTION:

I educate myself today, either by reading a book that I never read before, talking to a person I never talked to before, or viewing something I never viewed before. I light my fire.

## POINT TO PONDER:

When we educate ourselves or allow others to educate us, we turn on the lights in rooms in our heads that had been in the dark or only scarcely lit before. With every piece of education, the light glows brighter. Then, one day, the light is at its brightest. It is on that day that we realize that we still do not know a lot of our so-called area of expertise, because there is much that we will never know. This will keep us down to earth, regardless of the amount of education we receive. This is the path to wisdom.

# *November 27*

### GUIDING QUOTE:
*Difficulties are things that show a person what they are.*
~ EPICTETUS

## ACTION:
Whatever problem occurs today, I face it and find a solution, because I am a winner and I do not waver when I move toward my goal.

## POINT TO PONDER:
As long as everything is smooth, we cannot tell whether the people we deal with are the winning or the quitting kind. It takes a storm to find out who the drivers and who the defeatists are. This is the great advantage of hard times: they teache us whom we can count on and whom we cannot. At home, the weak ones will be those who only complicate matters instead of helping to find a solution. At work, we will detect the defeatists among those who always complain, rarely smile, and perceive work as a burden instead of a blessing.

# November 28

**GUIDING QUOTE:**

*We have two ears and one tongue so that we would listen more and talk less.*

~ DIOGENES

**ACTION:**

I listen deeply—with my ears, but also with my eyes, mind, and heart. I listen for the spoken and the unspoken, so that I learn beyond the trivial.

**POINT TO PONDER:**

It seems to be a modern-day fad to talk as much as you can. In restaurants, at meetings, in classrooms, people seem to want to top one another in assertiveness. What they often do not realize is that they give away more than just their abundance of words. They demonstrate a disinterest in what anyone else has to say, and an inflated ego so full of itself that nothing can deflate it. Above all, they refrain from learning, because their talking only fills their world with things they already know. This is something to think about.

# November 29

**GUIDING QUOTE:**

*Wise people, even though all laws were abolished, would still lead the same life.*

~ ARISTOPHANES

**ACTION:**

Today, I sharpen my self-discipline. I do not need rules and regulations to keep me in line. I do my duties diligently and devotedly.

**POINT TO PONDER:**

It was generally known in the village that atop the mountain there lived a wise man. One of the prominent villagers decided to make the long trip to meet this wise man and ask him some urgent questions. When he arrived, he was welcomed by an old servant. He said that he came to meet the wise man. The servant smiled and let him in. They walked and before the man knew it, he was led outside through the backdoor. When he asked where the holy man was and why he didn't meet him, the servant said, "You already have. You should see everyone you may meet in life, even if they appear plain and insignificant, as a wise holy man. If you do this, whatever problem you brought here today will be solved."

*(Adopted from John Suler, "Zen Stories to Tell Your Neighbors")*

# November 30

## GUIDING QUOTE:

*There are two things a person should never be angry at,
what they can help, and what they cannot.*

~ PLATO

## ACTION:

Whatever would drive me to get angry or upset today will not succeed. I study calmness and balance today. Anger makes me tired and ill.

## POINT TO PONDER:

The above adage makes a lot of sense. It demonstrates that there is actually never need for anger. When you can change something, you should not be angry, but work toward changing whatever is not right. When you cannot do anything about a situation, you do not have to be angry, because it is out of your control. Anger is a sentiment that hurts at least one person, but generally more. The carrier of the anger risks a heart attack, stroke, high blood pressure, and other stress-related symptoms that can deteriorate one's health. Many people are in prison for things they did in moments of blind anger. What is the point in ruining our lives?

*December*

# December 1

## GUIDING QUOTE:

*He that always gives way to others will end in having no principles of his own.*

~ AESOP

## ACTION:

Although I am not stubborn, I remain true to my beliefs and values. I walk a gentle middle path.

## POINT TO PONDER:

Yielding is one of those interesting phenomena that can be a great virtue or a painful weakness. Too little yielding makes one appear hard-nosed, arrogant, and difficult to get along with, resulting in isolation. Too much yielding creates the impression that the yielder is weak and spineless—an easy walkover. Neither of these two pictures suggests strong leadership, as people respect neither arrogance nor weakness in their leaders. It is an art to find the middle path. Those who do can count on great admiration and followership.

# December 2

**GUIDING QUOTE:**

*Discovery consists in seeing what everybody else has seen and thinking what nobody else has thought.*

~ ALBERT VON SZENT-GYÖRGI

**ACTION:**

I look with a novice mind at the things that I have seen many times before. I think creatively, either alone or on a team.

**POINT TO PONDER:**

Many people wonder if creative thinking can be taught. It may not be taught as a structured course, but it can be encouraged by actions of and in dialogue with wise people. When we expose ourselves to new environments, different people, and unfamiliar books, we open doors in our minds that had been closed. We start seeing things that others may have missed. It takes time and effort to create a creative mind, but the results are marvelous.

# December 3

### GUIDING QUOTE:

*Ideas are like rabbits. You get a couple and learn how to handle them, and pretty soon you have a dozen.*

~ JOHN STEINBECK

## ACTION:

Whatever stokes my creative fire is what I focus on today in every private moment I have. My ideas help me better my circumstances and those of loved ones.

## POINT TO PONDER:

Those who struggle with writer's or artist's block know how devastating the lack of fresh ideas can be. They also know how welcome new ideas can be. Inspiration feels like a rich stream of water that flows more rapidly the longer you look at it. It rejuvenates dullness and frees the individual from gloom. The most beautiful part of ideas is that they are contagious. One idea easily leads to another. Yet, it all has to start somehow. If you run into a drought in your idea supply, try a brief change of environment, or talk to an older, wiser person. Or simply do something out of the ordinary. It might work better than you would think.

# December 4

**GUIDING QUOTE:**

*Iron rusts from disuse; water loses its purity from stagnation, and in cold weather becomes frozen; even so does inaction sap the vigors of the mind.*

~ LEONARDO DA VINCI

**ACTION:**

I undertake action that makes me happy and satisfied. I do something nice for another, and make a new deposit on my emotional bank account.

**POINT TO PONDER:**

People who do not exercise their minds run a major risk of descending into a negative spiral of low self-esteem through senses of uselessness, boredom, and negativity. Laziness is only constructive if we use it as a foundation to invent something that will benefit others. Some lazy people think of ingenious ways to make their tasks easier. But those people form a rarefied group. The majority of lazy people remain unproductive, and therefore lose the precious vibrancy of mind. We should be leery of this danger.

# *December 5*

### GUIDING QUOTE:

*Never doubt that a small group of thoughtful, committed citizens can change the world. Indeed it is the only thing that ever has.*

~ MARGARET MEAD

### ACTION:

I influence my surroundings with positive vibes. I cherish the power of my team at work. United we stand.

### POINT TO PONDER:

There was once a general who was leading his forces into battle against an army ten times the size of his own. On the way to the battlefield, the troops stopped to pray for victory. The general held up a coin and told his troops, "If this coin lands with the heads on top, we'll win. If it's tails, we'll lose. Our fate is in the hands of the gods. Let's pray wholeheartedly." After a short prayer, the general tossed the coin. It landed heads up. The troops were overjoyed, went into the battle with high spirits, and won! The soldiers were exalted, "It's good to have the gods on our side! No one can change what they have determined." "Really?" The general showed them the coin with heads on both sides.

# December 6

## GUIDING QUOTE:

*For to be free is not merely to cast off one's chains,*
*but to live in a way that respects and enhances the freedom of others.*
~ NELSON MANDELA

## ACTION:

In everything I do, and with every decision I make, I question whether my steps cause discomfort and restrict freedom for others. If I find that to be the case, I seek other ways to reach my goals.

## POINT TO PONDER:

In our quest for freedom and progress, we often make decisions that favor ourselves, failing to consider the effects on others. We may not always go through life without harming others, but at the very least we can admit our failures in that regard. The progress that we make that also advantages others is much sweeter and more rewarding than what we do at others' expense.

# *December 7*

## GUIDING QUOTE:

*There is work that is work and there is play that is play; there is play that is work and work that is play. And in only one of these lies happiness.*

~ GELETT BURGESS

## ACTION:

Is my work play or is it drudgery? I contemplate on that. If I can see my work as play, I have succeeded. If I see it as drudgery, I start looking for something else to do.

## POINT TO PONDER:

There was once a member of a community service organization who stopped being part of his team. His friend decided to visit him and found him at home, sitting alone in front of the fireplace. No words were spoken. The visitor just picked one burning ember with the fire tongues out of the heap and laid it aside. Soon the fire of the ember died and it grew cold. When the friend decided to leave, he picked up the cold ember and placed it again in the middle of the fire. Immediately it began to glow with the warmth of the burning coals around it. The host said, "Thank you for reminding me of the importance of being part of something bigger than myself."

# December 8

## GUIDING QUOTE:
*He that is good for making excuses is seldom good for anything else.*
~ BENJAMIN FRANKLIN

## ACTION:

I am forthcoming about my actions. I refrain from making unnecessary excuses. If there is anything I need to do and want to do, I do it today.

## POINT TO PONDER:

It is easy to blame our lack of action or our failure to meet requirements on everyone and everything else except ourselves. Excuses, however, can become a habit, and one excuse leads to another. The more we make, the easier they become. Yet, we should realize that excuses justify only weakness of character and lack of reliability. Leaders do not make excuses, but face their tasks with determination. If we want to be leaders, we should stop making excuses.

# December 9

## GUIDING QUOTE:

*Jokes of the proper kind, properly told, can do more to enlighten questions of politics, philosophy, and literature than any number of dull arguments.*

~ ISAAC ASIMOV

## ACTION:

I take matters in a proper, lighthearted manner. I avoid arguments by taking the path of fun, kindness, and pleasant conversation. Yet, I show respect.

## POINT TO PONDER:

Holding grudges is a tiresome activity that negatively affects our health and our thinking. We can get so absorbed by anger and hate that it obstructs our performance and causes great opportunities that cross our paths to be lost. Remember this: even bad things serve a purpose. They are there to help us value the good things more. Why look at anything from a pessimistic perspective? We are blessed to be alive, and we are all winners by virtue of our existence. No need to fight or fuss. Life is good.

# $\mathscr{D}$ecember 10

*Stubbornness does have its helpful features.*
*You always know what you are going to be thinking tomorrow.*
~ GLEN BEAMAN

## ACTION:

I do not want to be stranded in eternally similar thoughts. Instead of being stubborn, I open myself to learn and be flexible, thus enriching my spirit.

## POINT TO PONDER:

Stubbornness is not only an arrogant trait, it is also shortsighted and can be the source of sheer suffering. Flexibility, on the other hand, can be a lifesaver. A Taoist story tells of an old man who accidentally fell into the river rapids leading to a mighty waterfall. Onlookers feared for his life. Miraculously, he came out alive and unharmed downstream from the falls. People asked him how he managed to survive. "I accommodated myself to the water, not the water to me. Without thinking, I allowed myself to be shaped by it. Plunging into the swirl, I came out with the swirl. This is how I survived."

# December 11

## GUIDING QUOTE:
*Some choices we live not only once but a thousand times over, remembering them for the rest of our lives.*
~ RICHARD BACH

## ACTION:
I think about the fact that my choices determine the rest of my life. I am cautious in making them.

## POINT TO PONDER:
One evening an old Cherokee told his grandson about a battle that goes on inside people. He said, "My son, the battle is between two wolves inside us all. One is Evil. It is anger, envy, jealousy, sorrow, regret, greed, arrogance, self-pity, guilt, resentment, inferiority, lies, false pride, superiority, and ego. The other is Good. It is joy, peace, love, hope, serenity, humility, kindness, benevolence, empathy, generosity, truth, compassion, and faith." The grandson thought about it for a minute and then asked his grandfather, "Which wolf wins?" The old Cherokee simply replied, "The one you feed."

# *December 12*

*Like an unchecked cancer, hate corrodes the personality and eats away its vital unity. Hate destroys a man's sense of values and his objectivity. It causes him to describe the beautiful as ugly and the ugly as beautiful, and to confuse the true with the false and the false with the true.*

~ MARTIN LUTHER KING, JR.

## ACTION:

Whatever malicious feelings I held toward others, today I let them go. I realize that malicious feelings distort my view and victimize me. I do not let that happen.

## POINT TO PONDER:

It seems so natural to gravitate to the similar. It also seems natural to mistrust—even hate—the different. This is a human trait. Yet, as old as this trait is, it needs to be adjusted. While we may never be able to spontaneously embrace everything and everybody, we should give everyone a fair chance to prove himself or herself. We should think on the opportunities we got in life, and how they were possible because others believed in us. Why not pay that forward?

# December 13

### GUIDING QUOTE:
*For every failure, there's an alternative course of action.
You just have to find it. When you come to a roadblock, take a detour.*

~ MARY KAY ASH

## ACTION:

I examine my failures, and review the ways in which I can take detours in order to transform them into successes.

## POINT TO PONDER:

Failure is an undervalued phenomenon. It is the best way to learn. Consider war heroes. What makes them heroes? Oftentimes it is the fact that they were wounded or captured, but managed to survive till they were freed. What makes a great cook? One who experimented a lot, ruined many recipes and pots, and became an expert in the end. We cannot become experts by only having successes. Success on a constant basis becomes a bore. It is the failure that keeps us alert and inspires us to explore new ground. Failure can therefore be seen as the spice of life.

# *December 14*

*Life is never boring, but some people choose to be bored…. Boredom is a choice.*
~ WAYNE W. DYER

## ACTION:

I do my duties, and after those are done, I devote my time to constructive leisure. I choose not to be bored.

## POINT TO PONDER:

Everyone has dealt with boredom at least once. Yet, there are many ways to end this state of being. For instance, you can 1) sit with your boredom and contemplate on it, until it passes—you will ultimately regain your sense of activity; 2) surround yourself with do-ers—their busy-ness can inspire you; 3) alternate between reading and writing—the secret here is to break the rhythm of a regular action; 4) be irrational—step away from an overly organized lifestyle for a change; 5) connect with an old friend—there is always something fun to discover there; or 6) get out and play—check nature out.

*(Posted on* Zenhabits.net *by Todd Goldfarb)*

Each of these strategies can help you to lose that dreary sense that overwhelms you when bored, and get you back on track.

# December 15

### GUIDING QUOTE:
*The best education in the world is that got by struggling to get a living.*
~ WENDELL PHILLIPS

## ACTION:

I am not disheartened by my struggles toward advancement, but realize that struggling is an asset in life.

## POINT TO PONDER:

A man found a cocoon for a butterfly. One day a small opening appeared. The man watched the butterfly as it struggled to force its body through the little hole. Then it appeared to be stuck. The man decided to help the butterfly and gently cut open the cocoon. The butterfly emerged easily, but it had a swollen body and shriveled wings. The man waited for it to take on its correct proportions, but nothing changed. The butterfly was never able to fly. In his kindness and haste, the man did not realize that the butterfly's struggle to get through the small opening of the cocoon is nature's way of forcing fluid from the body of the butterfly into its wings so that it would be ready for flight. In life we all need to struggle sometimes to make us strong.

# December 16

## GUIDING QUOTE:

*Either you think—or else others have to think for you and take power from you, pervert and discipline your natural tastes, civilize and sterilize you.*

~ F. SCOTT FITZGERALD

## ACTION:

I think for myself today. I consider my circumstances and contemplate where I want to be in five years. I consider the roads I have to take, and work toward achieving my goals. I do not let any one-size-fits-all thoughts paralyze me.

## POINT TO PONDER:

It may strike us as funny, but many people do not think for themselves when it comes to the ultimate scene of their lives. They consider small steps, but leave the major decisions to their workplace or their government. This is victimized thinking. Yet, we do not have to be victims if we do not want to. We can think for ourselves and choose the paths that we prefer for our future. We can inspire ourselves by reflecting on the lives of those we admire: they achieved their goals through thinking, and then acting.

# December 17

*Tension is who you think you should be. Relaxation is who you are.*

~ CHINESE PROVERB

## ACTION:

I work diligently to alleviate my struggles toward advancement, and am content with who I am.

## POINT TO PONDER:

One day when Buddha was teaching a group of people, he was verbally abused by an angry bystander. The Buddha listened patiently while the stranger vented his rage, and then he said to the group and the stranger, "If someone gives a gift to another person, who then chooses to decline it, who owns the gift? The giver or the person who refuses to accept the gift?" "The giver," answered the group. "Any fool can see that," added the angry stranger. "Then it follows," said the Buddha, "whenever a person tries to abuse us, or to unload their anger on us, we can each choose to decline or to accept the abuse. By our personal response to the abuse from another, we can choose who owns and keeps the bad feelings."

# December 18

## GUIDING QUOTE:

*Freedom is the recognition that no single person, no single authority or government has a monopoly on the truth, but that every individual life is infinitely precious, that every one of us put in this world has been put there for a reason and has something to offer.*

~ RONALD REAGAN

## ACTION:

I have a lot to offer. I take the freedom to define what it is that I have to offer—to the world, to my workplace, to my family, and to myself.

## POINT TO PONDER:

Life is beautiful. We all are beautiful. We are unique, and we have so many qualities, regardless of how, when, or where we were born. We need not be disheartened by our discomforts, because everyone has some. We should rather focus on our distinguished capacities to contribute to the well-being of life on earth. If we all do that, the world is saved!

# *December 19*

### GUIDING QUOTE:

*Everyone chases after happiness, not noticing that happiness is right at their heels.*

~ BERTOLT BRECHT

### ACTION:

I am peaceful and content. I am happy and grateful for existing. Here is good, there is good.

### POINT TO PONDER:

An old cat saw a kitten chasing its tail and asked, "Why are you chasing your tail?" The kitten replied, "I've been attending cat philosophy school and I have learned that the most important thing for a cat is happiness, and that happiness is my tail. Therefore, I am chasing it, and when I catch it, I shall have happiness forever." The wise old cat replied, "I wasn't lucky enough to go to school, but as I've gone through life, I too have realized that the most important thing for a cat is happiness, and indeed that it is located in my tail. The difference I've found though is that whenever I chase after it, it keeps running away from me, but when I go about my business and live my life, it just seems to follow after me wherever I go."

# December 20

## GUIDING QUOTE:

*If your head is intact you can have a thousand turbans.*

~ INDIAN PROVERB

## ACTION:

Material gain comes if I take good care of the most important thing: my health. I do what I need to do to live healthier, mentally and physically.

## POINT TO PONDER:

We worry too much about appearances and forget the things that really matter, until it is almost too late. We should set our priorities straight and think on all those who have gone before us and made the same mistakes. Time and again we see that people who considered themselves so important pass away, and the world forgets them almost instantly. Why should we, therefore, not take good care of ourselves, and then, perhaps, work on less important matters?

# *December 21*

*Not everything that can be counted counts,*
*and not everything that counts can be counted.*

~ ALBERT EINSTEIN

## ACTION:

I give kindness, attention, support, encouragement, and love. These virtues cannot be counted, but they are most precious to me, and probably to others as well.

## POINT TO PONDER:

Gandhi was boarding a train one day with a number of companions and followers, when his shoe fell from his foot and disappeared in the gap between the train and platform. Unable to retrieve it, he took off his other shoe and threw it down by the first. Responding to the puzzlement of his fellow travelers, Gandhi explained that a poor person who finds a single shoe is no better off—what's really helpful is finding a pair.

# December 22

## GUIDING QUOTE:

*When we lose one blessing, another is often most unexpectedly given in its place.*
~ C. S. LEWIS

## ACTION:

I do not look back on lost chances, because I know that something better will come along.

## POINT TO PONDER:

One day a small rat surfaced from his nest to find himself between the paws of a huge sleeping lion, which immediately awoke and seized the rat. The rat pleaded with the fierce beast to be set free, and the lion, being very noble and wise, and in no need of such small prey, agreed to let the relieved rat go on his way. Some days later, a hunter had laid a trap for the lion, and it duly caught him, so that the lion was trussed up in a strong net, helpless, with nothing to do but wait for the hunter to return. But it was the rat who came along next, and seeing the lion in need of help, promptly set about gnawing through the net, which soon began to unravel, setting the great lion free. Giving a blessing always results in getting an even bigger one in return.

# December 23

## GUIDING QUOTE:

*Everything can be taken from a man but…the last of the human freedoms—to choose one's attitude in any given set of circumstances, to choose one's own way.*

~ VICTOR FRANKL

## ACTION:

I can choose to see my life and work as great, mediocre or bad. I choose the first and simply live it.

## POINT TO PONDER:

We can determine our own perspective on life. There was an old lady who cried all the time. She had two daughters: the oldest was married to an umbrella salesman, and the younger one to a noodle vendor. When the sun shone, she cried for her oldest daughter, because no one needed an umbrella when it was sunny. When it rained, she cried for her youngest daughter, because in rainy weather noodles could not dry. One day the crying lady met a monk, who asked her what her problem was. Upon hearing the problem, the monk suggested she shift her thoughts and think of the oldest daughter on rainy days and the youngest on sunny days. She never cried again.

# *December 24*

**GUIDING QUOTE:**

*Emancipate yourselves from mental slavery;*
*none but ourselves can free our minds!*

~ BOB MARLEY

**ACTION:**

Am I merely thinking the way I was taught to think? Can I step out of mental slavery and start thinking for myself? Do I dare to see the world with my own eyes, heart and mind? Today I dare.

**POINT TO PONDER:**

Many people think that thinking is something for scholars, meditators, and gurus. That is not true. Thinking is an active pursuit that we should all engage in regularly—not merely thinking as an extension to what we have always learned, but along new paths that have not been treaded before. Most people go through the daily motions without contemplating whether they engage in what they really want to and can do, or whether they are submitting to mental slavery. We can make a difference by starting to think for ourselves!

# December 25

## GUIDING QUOTE:

*A poor person isn't he who has little, but he who needs a lot.*

~ GERMAN PROVERB

## ACTION:

How much am I willing to strive for? What am I willing to strive for? Why? I examine my goals and wonder if they are necessary. I do not need a lot to be rich.

## POINT TO PONDER:

People who need much are constantly trying to fill the holes in their minds and hearts. They purchase and gather to numb their discontentment rather than to be satisfied. They miss something, and to suppress that feeling, they need increasingly more, yet it is never enough, because the need increases as the discontentment does. It is much better to face the root of our needy behavior, and do something about it. This is how we can regain our balance and natural wealth.

# December 26

## GUIDING QUOTE:

*Loud speech, profusion of words, and possessing skillfulness in expounding scriptures are merely for the enjoyment of the learned. They do not lead to liberation.*

~ ADI SHANKARACHARYA

## ACTION:

Why would I always want to be heard? It is better for me to listen and learn—not only from the words, but also about the one who utters them. Today, I listen and observe.

## POINT TO PONDER:

Many people talk infinitely in order to create the impression that they are enlightened. However, enlightenment does not lie in the use of high words, as the quote states above, nor does it lie in extreme intelligence. There is a difference between intelligence and being liberated. One attains liberation more easily through contemplating, helping, understanding, listening, giving, and observing. We should talk less and listen more.

# December 27

## GUIDING QUOTE:

*When you wholeheartedly adopt a "with all your heart" attitude and go out with the positive principle, you can do incredible things.*

~ NORMAN VINCENT PEALE

## ACTION:

I make it a point to do something good, and talk to someone wise today. Kindness and wisdom are today's guides.

## POINT TO PONDER:

A very old lady looked in the mirror one morning. She had three remaining hairs on her head, and being a positive soul, she said, "I think I'll braid my hair today." She braided her three hairs, and had a great day. Some days later she saw that she had only two hairs remaining. "Hmm, two hairs—I fancy a center parting today." She duly parted her two hairs, and had a great day. A week later, she had just one hair left on her head. "One hair, huh?" she mused. "I know—a ponytail will be perfect." Again she had a great day. The next morning she looked in the mirror. She was completely bald. "Finally bald, huh?" she said to herself. "How wonderful! I won't have to waste time doing my hair any more."

# December 28

## GUIDING QUOTE:

*Let us not take ourselves too seriously. None of us has a monopoly on wisdom.*
~ QUEEN ELIZABETH

## ACTION:

I make it a point today to laugh about myself. Even though I do not deliberately set out to err, I am sure I can catch myself making a mistake, or thinking something strange. I do not let that aggravate me.

## POINT TO PONDER:

People who take themselves too seriously become hard to get along with. They lose their sense of humor and concentrate on achievements to the exclusion of all else. They get so stressed that their life may turn into a volcano, continuously on the verge of eruption. Yet, even the wisest and richest of the world have made their fair share or mistakes. Mistakes are the beauty spots of life. Without them, life would be dull. Let us forgive ourselves everyday and start anew.

# December 29

*Each problem that I solved became a rule which
served afterwards to solve other problems.*

~ RENÉ DESCARTES

**ACTION:**

The knowledge I gain by solving the problems of today will become useful for future challenges. Today, I face challenges that I have avoided.

**POINT TO PONDER:**

We learn from our failures. We also learn from solving problems. Life can be seen as a sequence of problems, but also as a chain of learning opportunities. We grow with every problem we encounter, and use the experience to either prevent similar issues in the future, or to use it creatively in other issues. The problem-solving process sharpens our creativity and our mind. So why complain when we face challenges?

# December 30

## GUIDING QUOTE:

*What shall it profit a man if he gains the whole world but loses his soul?*

~ JESUS CHRIST

## ACTION:

I focus on love. Love for my family, co-workers, and all those I encounter, even if I do not know them. All life is connected. I celebrate that.

## POINT TO PONDER:

These days, we are so programmed to gather as much as possible that we forget to really live. What was once a quest for a decent life is now a race toward destructive greed. We want it all, while less would do just as well. We behave like the boy who put his hand into a pitcher full of sweets. He grasped as many as he could possibly hold, but when he tried to pull out his hand, he was prevented from doing so by the neck of the pitcher. Unwilling to lose his sweets, and yet unable to withdraw his hand, he burst into tears and bitterly lamented his disappointment. A bystander said to him, "Be satisfied with half the quantity, and you will readily draw out your hand." We should not grasp for too much at once.

# *December 31*

**GUIDING QUOTE:**
*All conditioned things are impermanent.*
*Work out your own salvation with diligence.*
~ BUDDHA

**ACTION:**
I contemplate on the purpose of life in general, and my life specifically. I attach myself neither to victory nor to defeat. They are all impermanent.

**POINT TO PONDER:**
A farmer worked the land with his two sons. They were happy, but one day the father passed away. After the funeral, the sons rearranged the father's belongings and found a small box with two rings. One was gold, set with a large diamond stone; the other was a simple silver ring. The oldest son, always very materialistic, quickly thought of a reason to get the expensive ring. He claimed that, being the oldest, he should have the ring as a family piece. The younger brother, a peaceful person, agreed. When life continued, the older brother got back to his dissatisfied ways, while the younger remained his calm, balanced self. One day he looked more closely at his silver ring and noticed an engraving inside: "This, too, shall pass." He understood and smiled.